THREE
REFORMERS

THREE REFORMERS

LUTHER — DESCARTES — ROUSSEAU

BY

JACQUES MARITAIN

GREENWOOD PRESS, PUBLISHERS
WESTPORT, CONNECTICUT

Originally published in 1950
by Charles Scribner's Sons

First Greenwood Reprinting 1970

SBN 8371-2825-0

PRINTED IN UNITED STATES OF AMERICA

CONTENTS

LUTHER

DESCARTES

ROUSSEAU

To
MY MOTHER

LUTHER

or

THE ADVENT OF THE SELF

LUTHER

or

THE ADVENT OF THE SELF

Si filius Dei es, mitte te deorsum (Matth. iv, 6).
"The Prototype of modern times" (Eichte).

§ I. THE AUTHOR'S INTENTION

1. WE are bound to the past in the intellectual
order as in every other, and if we were to forget that
we are animals which are specifically *political*, we
should be surprised to discover how *historically* we
think, how traditional we are, even when we are
claiming to make all things new. It is, then, right
that we should go some distance into the past in our
search for the roots and first germinative principle
of the ideas which rule the world to-day. It is when
an idea appears above ground, when it is big with the
future, that it has the greatest interest for us and we
can best grasp its real significance.

I am not, however, proposing an historical study.
I shall ask of history only the manifestation, in certain
representative types, of the spiritual principles which
it is most necessary for us to distinguish.

N.B.—Numbers refer to notes at the end of the book; signs, to notes
at the foot of the page.

2. Three men, each for very different reasons, dominate the modern world, and govern all the problems which torment it: a reformer of religion, a reformer of philosophy, and a reformer of morality, —Luther, Descartes, and Rousseau. They are in very truth the begetters of what M. Gabriel Séailles called the modern conscience. I do not speak of Kant, who stands at the meeting of the intellectual streams springing from these three men, and created, so to say, the academic structure of modern thought.

I shall consider Luther, not to study him exhaustively and as the founder of Protestantism, but to bring out certain features in the character of that enemy of philosophy which are of consequence to our philosophical battles. After all, it would be astonishing if the extraordinary loss of balance induced in the Christian mind by heresy had not had the most important repercussions in all spheres, particularly in that of the speculative and practical reason. By the very fact that the Lutheran revolution bore on religion, on that which governs all human activity, it was bound to change most profoundly the attitude of the human soul and of speculative thought confronted with reality.

§ II. A SPIRITUAL DRAMA

3. Martin Luther, strong summoner of the great undefined powers which lie dormant in the heart of the creature of flesh, was gifted with a nature at once realistic and lyrical, powerful, impulsive, brave and sad, sentimental and morbidly sensitive. Vehement as he was, there yet was in him kindness,

generosity, tenderness, and, with all, unbroken pride
and peevish vanity. What was lacking in him was
force of intellect. If by intelligence we mean capacity
to grasp the universal, to discern the essential, to
follow with docility the wanderings and refinements
of reality, Luther was not intelligent, but limited,—
stubborn, especially. But he had the understanding
of the particular and practical to an amazing degree,
and an astute and lively ingenuity, skill to detect
even in others, the art of finding a thousand ways out
of a difficulty and crushing his opponent—in short,
all the resources of what philosophers call the
"cogitative," the "particular reason."

He entered religion, if we may accept his own story,
as the result of a feeling of terror occasioned, first
by the death of one of his friends who was killed in a
duel, then by a violent storm in which he nearly died.
He was "not so much drawn as carried away,"
non tam tractus quam raptus. He seems to have been
exact and perhaps fervent[1] in the early days of his
religious life, but he was always anxious and troubled. [2]
At a time when the general level of clerical life in
Germany had fallen wretchedly low, he had declared for the current of reform, and, as he says,
did not let cobwebs grow on his snout when there
were abuses to be stormed at. At twenty-five he was
professor at the University of Wittenberg; at twenty-
nine, doctor of sacred theology; and the duty of
teaching, so imprudently given to a man so restless,
threw him at once into the acrid atmosphere of
human controversy and transferred his zeal into
arrogance and presumption. [3] From Scholasticism
hastily and imperfectly studied, he had derived

nothing but an arsenal of false ideas and vague
theological notions, and a disconcerting skill in
specious argument.

What he became later must not prevent our imagining what he may first have been as a Catholic,
as a religious, sincerely setting all his natural impetuosity to that pursuit of perfection which he had
vowed. On the contrary, nothing is more instructive
than to try to picture what that young religious may
have been. From his own witness and the studies of
Denifle and Grisar I note here two things in the
inner life of Brother Martin.

First, he seems to have sought in the spiritual life
chiefly what authors call sensible consolations, and
to have been desperately attached to that experimental
savouring of piety, that assurance in feeling, which
God sends to souls to draw them to Himself, but takes
from them when He wills, and which are only means.
For Luther, on the other hand, the whole point was
to *feel* himself in a state of grace—as if grace in itself
were an object of sensation! Did not the theological
thesis that grace is infused into the soul at the very
moment when sin is effaced "drive him almost to
despair of God, of all that God is, and all that He
possesses",* because he did not experience in himself that perfect pureness of grace? Thus in a disturbed
and carnal soul a strong mystical homesickness dis-
torted all the teaching of spiritual writers, and turned
to a brutal craving to enjoy its own sanctity. Luther
tasted of the hidden fruits of Christ's grace; he

* Sermon of 27th December, 1514. Weim., I, 43, 5-12; IV, 665,
15-22. (Denifle, *Luther et le luthéranisme*, ed. Paquier, 2nd ed.,
1913, II, 400, suggests 1515.)

entered the spiritual garden of the Church; I am even inclined to believe that he went a considerable way; but from the very beginning his inner life was disorientated. The human subject, and that in the highest and most subtle order, became in fact for him of more concern than God.[4]

Then, and as a result of the same vicious disposition, he relied on his own strength alone to attain to Christian virtue and perfection, trusting to his own efforts, his penances, the works of his will, far more than to grace. Thus he practised the very Pelagianism with which he was to charge Catholics, from which he himself was never really to be free. In his spiritual life he was, in practice, a Pharisee relying on his works,[5] as his scrupulous fidgetiness shows,—for he had at that time many of the characteristics of the scrupulous: he blamed himself for all the first involuntary impressions of the senses as if they were sins, and strove to reach a holiness which should not betray the least sign of human frailty. . . . Moreover he was at the same time tormented by the pride with which the soul in such a state beholds itself. If the sacrament of penance does away his sin, he is at once better than everyone else! "I could not understand, in my madness, how, after I had repented and confessed, it could be right for me to think myself a sinner like others and not to prefer myself above the rest."*

Then came the night, that *night of sense* whose darkness is proportioned to the soul's need to be emptied of self. Martin Luther has lost all sensible consolation, he is plunged in a sea of agonies, he sees with that

* Commentary on Chap, IV. of the *Epistle to the Romans*, Folio 1446, Ficker, II. 109.

pitiless clearness which God gives in such cases the vanity and perversity filling his human heart; the whole building of perfection which he has tried to raise with his own hands seems to collapse on him, to turn against him in reproach. It might be the night of purification, and the time, perhaps, to choose his eternal destiny. What does he do? Does he forsake himself? Does he cast himself on God? Does he repeat to his troubled heart that great saying of Augustine: "Vis fugere a Deo, fuge in Deum"? He gave up praying and threw himself into activity to escape. He tried to drown his anguish in a sea of toil.

"I need two secretaries," he writes in 1516 to Lang, prior of Erfurt. "I do practically nothing all day long but write letters . . . I am Preacher of the Convent and in the Refectory; I am called daily to preach in the parish, I am Director of Studies and Vicar of the district, and thereby elevenfold Prior;* I am responsible for the fish-ponds at Leitzkau; I am agent at Torgau in the suit for Herzberg parish church; I give lectures on St. Paul, I am collecting notes on the Psalter. I rarely have time to recite my Office and say Mass."[6]

Now he had hardly strength to stand against the malignant fevers of nature. "I am," he will admit three years later, "I am but a man prone to let himself be swept off his feet by society, drunkenness, the movements of the flesh . . ."[7] And again in a sermon of the same period on the state of marriage, "What is needed to live in continence is not in me." Is it then that at the decisive moment of his crisis he falls into some grave outward failing? Apparently not.

* In the sense that he had eleven convents to guide.

But inwardly he fell; he despaired of grace. When a man begins to know the wounds and wretchedness of the sons of Adam, the serpent whispers in his ear: "Be content to be what you are, spoiled angel, misbegotten creature; your business is to do ill, since your very being is bad." A spiritual temptation pre-eminently. Luther makes that act of perverse resignation; he gives up the fight; he declares that the fight is impossible. Submerged by sin on all sides, or by what he thinks to be sin, he lets himself go with the tide. And he comes to the practical conclusion: *Concupiscence cannot be conquered.*[8]

4. So far we have only the classical story, if I may dare to call it so, of the fallen monk.[9] Doubtless; but notice:—You think he is crushed? He is on the point of breaking free, under full sail for sanctity. It is now that Luther the reformer appears, that he discovers the Gospel, that the Gospel frees him, that Christian liberty is revealed to him. What does he see in the Gospel and St. Paul? Exactly what we were just taking for a confession of despair: *Concupiscence is unconquerable.* The resignation of the man, the pessimist; abandonment to animality, a preface to the optimistic surrender of Jean-Jacques and the false *sincerity* of unmoral asceticism. Concupiscence Luther identifies with original sin. Original sin is always in us, ineffaceable; it has made us radically bad, corrupt in the very essence of our nature. God commanded the impossible when He gave us His law. But now Christ has paid for us and His justice redeems us. He is just in our stead. Justification is wholly exterior to us and we are still sin to our very bones: it infuses no new life into us, it

simply covers us as with a cloak. There is nothing
for us to do to be saved. On the contrary, to want to
co-operate with the divine action is a lack of faith, a
denial of the Blood of Christ, and damnation. [9A]

From henceforth "Heaven opens."[10] Good-bye
to torments and remorse! *Absolute uselessness of works;
salvation by faith alone*, that is to say, by a burst of
hope. *Pecca fortiter et crede firmius.*[11] Sin courageously,
believe more firmly than ever and you will be saved.

Now Luther has a doctrine; now he heads a school,[12]
is master and prophet; and he can win over to his
theology all the greed, all the impatient sensuality,
the putrid fermentation, mixed with hopes of reform
fed more by humanism and learning than by supernatural faith, in the Germany of his day. His doctrine, clearly, is born chiefly of his own inward experience. We must, no doubt, take account of his
reading of St Augustine, ill understood; of the
influence of the conflict between conventual and
observant Augustinians which Grisar points out;
and especially of the action of the theological stream
called Augustinian.[13] But all that is secondary. For
that soul, now devastated, it is faith saving without
works, no longer theological faith[14] but a merely
human impulse of trust, aping in its despair the
virtue of faith,—it is faith-trust which must now
ensure the state of spiritual comfort no longer ex-
pected of the perceptible tasting of grace, but none
the less always essentially aimed at.[15] What Luther's
doctrine especially expresses is Luther's interior states,
spiritual adventures, and individual history. Unable
to conquer himself, he transforms his necessities into
theological truths, and his own actual case into a

universal law. And, withal, longing for the moral
security and the liberty of the sons of the kingdom,
he frees himself—he thinks he frees himself—from all
the tortures of his conscience by despairing once for
all of all works and casting himself, as he is, on trust
in Christ. He is only an inverted Pharisee, a runaway
victim of scruples.

The unhappy man thinks he no longer trusts in
himself, but in God alone. Yet by refusing to admit
that man can share really and within himself in the
justice of Jesus Christ and in His grace—which,
according to him, is always external to us and cannot
produce in us any vital act[16]—he shuts himself up
for ever in his self, he withdraws from himself all
support but his self, he sets up as a doctrine what had
first been nothing but the sin of an individual, he
places the centre of his religious life not in God but in
man. At the moment when, after the storms let loose
by the business of the Indulgences, he raises his self
in the world against the Pope and the Church, within
himself his interior life is completely overturned.

5. We know what followed; it was inevitable.
Amidst the starts and storms of a life consumed by
activity, experiencing the unheard-of success of resistance to the power of the Church and the complete
upheaval of Germany and Christendom, yet keeping
a certain homesickness for a better fate, Luther yields
to the forces of instinct, he becomes subject to the
law of the flesh, following a progress which we may be
permitted to remark in the series of portraits of him,
the last of which are surprisingly bestial.[17] Anger,
calumny, hatred and lying, love of beer and wine,
obsession with filth and obscenity,[18]—it all pours out

in a flood, and always in "spirit" and in "truth",
in life, in Gospel holiness, in the good odour of
Christian liberty.

Now he preaches from the pulpit: "Just as I have
no power not to be a man, so it does not lie in my
power to live without a woman."* He gathers sensuality everywhere, on the pretext of alleviating
intolerable burdens and of facilitating virtue; he
broadcasts in convents of women, to urge the nuns to
find husbands, exhortations the product of a foul imagination, and impossible to transcribe.[19] "We are all
saints," he adds.† If there is talk of prayer and fast-
ing, and mortification, "even dogs and pigs can
almost practise that kind of sanctity every day."[20]
Does his conscience gnaw him again after that? It
is the business of faith-trust to make it let go, and
that is not always easy. Meanwhile, what is to be
done when troubles are too serious, when the devil
comes and pokes the fire of conscience to annoy a
man? "Seek out the society of your boon com-
panions, drink, play, talk bawdy, and amuse yourself. One must, sometimes, even commit a sin out
of hate and contempt for the devil, so as not to give
him the chance to make one scrupulous over mere
nothings; if one is too frightened of sinning one is
lost." "Oh! If I could find some really good sin
that would give the devil a toss."[21] It is also good
to put oneself in a violent temper, to imagine the Pope
with his "ulcers and vermin."† If one can't pray
in such a condition, at least one can curse.[22]

* Erl., 20, 58; Weim., X, P. II, 276, 14–1. (Sermon on marriage, 1522.)
† Erl., 60, 107–108.

But what should be observed here is not the result but the cause. That cause is hidden in Luther's spiritual life, and one might say that that immense disaster for humanity, the Protestant Reformation, was only the effect of an interior trial which turned out badly in a religious who lacked humility. It was in the heights of the spirit that he first fell, that he gave battle and was conquered. The play was staged *in acie mentis*, at the highest point of the soul. Luther says that he saw and defied innumerable demons who threatened him and argued with him. In origin and principle the drama of the Reformation was a spiritual drama, a battle of the soul.

It was fitting that it should be so and that the seed of the anti-Christian revolution should be brought into the world by a man vowed to perfection, consecrated to God, marked eternally with the character of the priesthood, who would pervert the Gospel. *Accipe potestatem sacrificandi pro vivis et mortuis.* Ah! We understand only too well why on the day of his ordination he wished that the earth would swallow him* at these words of the bishop; why he was seized with such horror at the beginning of the Canon of the Mass that he would have fled from the altar if the Novice Master had not held him back.† "His heart bled," he said, "whenever he read the Canon of the Mass."‡

Maurras is fond of quoting the proverb: A fish rots first at the head. If we can say with M. Seillière, speaking of Jean-Jacques Rousseau, that the modern

* Kuhn: *Luther, sa vie son œuvre* (Paris, 1883), I, 56.
† Coll., III, 169; Weim., *Tischreden*, III, 411, 4–9.
‡ *Lauterbachs Tagebuch*, 18. (With reference Gabriel Biel.)

world derives from a *mystical heresy*, how much more true is this of Luther than of Jean-Jacques! Everything begins in the spirit, and all the great events of modern history have been formed in the inmost soul of a few men, in the life of that *nous* which, as Aristotle says, is nothing at all as to volume and mass. The cell where Luther argued with the Devil, the stove against which Descartes had his famous dream, the corner of the Bois de Vincennes where Jean-Jacques soaked his waistcoat under an oak on discovering the goodness of the natural man,—those are the birthplaces of the modern world.[23]

§ III   THE INDIVIDUAL AND THE PERSON

6. What first impresses us in Luther's character is *egocentrism:* something much subtler, much deeper, and much more serious, than egoism; a metaphysical egoism. Luther's self becomes practically the centre of gravity of everything, especially in the spiritual order. And Luther's self is not only his passing quarrels and passions, it has a representative value; it is the self of the created being, the incommunicable stuff of the human individual. The Reformation unbridled the human self in the spiritual and religious order, as the Renaissance (I mean the hidden spirit of the Renaissance) unbridled the human self in the order of natural and sensible activities.

After Luther decided to refuse obedience to the Pope and break with the communion of the Church, his self is henceforth supreme, despite his interior agonies which increased until the end. Every "external" rule, every "heteronomy", as Kant said, becomes then an intolerable insult to his "Christian liberty".

"I do not admit," he writes in June 1522, "that my doctrine can be judged by anyone, even by the angels. He who does not receive my doctrine cannot be saved."*
"Luther's self," wrote Moehler, "was in his opinion the centre round which all humanity should gravitate; he made himself the universal man in whom all should find their model. Let us make no bones about it, he put himself in the place of Jesus Christ."

7. As we have already noticed, Luther's doctrine is itself only a universalization of his self, a projection of his self into the world of eternal truths. From this point of view, what distinguishes the father of Protestantism from the other great heresiarchs is that they started first from a dogmatic error, from a false doctrinal view; whatever their psychological origins may have been, the cause of their heresies is a deviation of the intelligence, and their own fortunes only count insofar as they conditioned that deviation. It is quite different with Luther. What counts is his life, his history. Doctrine comes as an extra. Lutheranism is not a system worked out by Luther; it is the overflow of Luther's individuality. It will be the same with Rousseau; the procedure is essentially romantic. It is that which explains the "Reformer's" immense influence on the German people. That is why a Lutheran like Seeberg cannot contain his admiration of that truly *daimonic* man, as he calls him, at that colossal figure of the superhuman which it is blasphemous to presume to judge. The question is, whether every flood is beautiful and good of itself,

* Erl., 28, 144.

and whether a river deserves our gratitude for simply spreading over the fields.

If you are looking for the translation of this ego-centrism into dogma, you will find it in some of the most noticeable characteristics of the Lutheran theology. What is the Lutheran dogma of the certainty of salvation* but the transference to the human individual and his subjective state of that absolute assurance in the divine promises which was formerly the privilege of the Church and her mission?† Because God was her centre, the Catholic soul needed to know nothing with perfect certainty except the mysteries of the faith, and that God is love and is merciful. And if He sent her tokens of His love, she used these experimental signs[24] less to probe herself and judge of her state before God than to live the imperfect certainties of hope with greater strength, certainties all the dearer that the conscience dare hardly receive the confession of them. But without perfect certainty of her state of grace the heretical soul could not exist without breaking for agony, because she has become the centre and seeks her salvation in the justice with which she covers herself,

---

* "But yet there was something very special about the secret of this justifying faith, and that was, that it did not consist in a general belief in the Saviour, in His mysteries and promises, but in believing most certainly, each in his own heart, that all our sins had been forgiven us. Luther incessantly repeated that we are justified as soon as we believe with certainty that we are justified; and the certainty which he required was not merely that moral certainty which is based on reasonable motives and excludes agitation and trouble, but an absolute certainty, an infallible certainty, in which the sinner must believe he is justified with the same faith with which he believes that Jesus Christ came into the world." (Bossuet: *Hist. des Var.*, I, 8.) So Lutheranism seems to be a sort of "mind cure" in the order of eternal salvation.

† See the very judicious note by M. Paquier on this point. (Denifle-Paquier, III, 428-9.)

not in the abyss of the mercies of Another, Who made her.

Why does the doctrine of salvation absorb all the Lutheran theology, if it be not because the human self has become in actual fact the chief preoccupation of that theology?[25] For Luther, one question towers above all the rest: to escape the judicial wrath of the Almighty in spite of the invincible concupiscence which poisons our nature. The truth is, that if it is essentially important that we should save ourselves, it is less to escape the devil than to see the face of God, and less to save our own being from the fire than from love of Him Whom we love more than ourselves. "Domine ostende nobis Patrem, et sufficit nobis." Catholic theology is ordered to God, and it is, by that very fact, a science chiefly speculative.* Lutheran theology is for the creature; that is why it aims above all at the practical end to be attained. Luther, who drives charity away and keeps servile fear, so far as he has any, makes the science of divine things revolve round human corruption.

Is not the salvation of man, however, the work of God and His Christ? Beware: in the Lutheran theology grace is always wholly extrinsic to ourselves,† man is walled up in his nature and can never receive in himself the seeds of true participation in the divine life, nor (child of wrath as he is) can he produce a substantially supernatural act. A flavour of the devil mingles with everything he does. "I say that

* It is speculative and practical *at the same time* from its higher unity, but it is primarily and chiefly speculative. (Cf. *Summa Theol.*, I, 1, 4.)

† For Luther, grace is nothing else than the simple *exterior favour* of God. Cf. Weim., VIII, 106, 22; Erl., 63, 123, etc. Denifle-Paquier, III, pp. 77, 213, 217.

whether it be in man or devil, the spiritual powers
have been not only corrupted by sin, but absolutely
destroyed; so that there is now nothing in them
but a depraved reason and a will that is the enemy
and opponent of God, whose only thought is war
against God."* "True piety, piety of value in God's
eyes, is found in works which are foreign to us (those
of Christ), not in our own."† Can then the act of
justifying faith, if it comes from us, come also from God
and from Christ acting in us? In fact it is ourselves,
and we alone, who catch at Christ's cloak to "cover
all our shame with it," and use that "*skill* to leap
from our sin on to Christ's justice, and hence to be as
certain of possessing Christ's piety as we are of having
our own bodies."‡ The Pelagianism of despair!
In fine, it is for man himself to work his own redemption by driving himself to a desperate trust in Christ.[26]
Human nature will only have to throw off as an empty
theological accessory the cloak of a meaningless grace
and turn its faith-trust on to itself,§ and it will become that pleasant liberated beast whose continual
and infallible progress delights the universe to-day.

And thus in the person of Luther and in his doctrine,
we are present—and that on the level of the spirit
and religious life—at the Advent of the Self.‖

* *In Galat.* (1535), Weim., XL, P. I, 293, 24–27.
† Erl., 15, 60 (1527).
‡ *Tischreden* (1531–1532), ed. Preger, 1888, p. 41. Cf. Cordatus,
ed. Wrampelmeyer, p. 131, n.573; Colloquia, ed. Bindseil, II, 298, 3–7.
§ Cf. Dilthey: *Das natürliche System der Geisteswissenschaften*, Arch. f.
Gesch. der Phil., t. V, p. 377ff (and p. 285).
‖ Obviously we are considering here only the *spiritual principle* of
modern individualism. That in other orders—social, intellectual,
æsthetic,—this latter had already made its appearance long before
the Reformation, and that the Lutheran revolution to a degree drove
back individualism by its communal or gregarious character and

8. But then, surely Luther's case shows us precisely
one of the problems against which modern man
beats in vain. It is the problem of *individualism and
personality*. Look at the Kantian shrivelled up in his
autonomy, the Protestant tormented by concern for
his inward liberty, the Nietzschean giving himself
curvature of the spine in his effort to jump beyond
good and evil, the Freudian cultivating his complexes
and sublimating his libido, the thinker preparing
an unpublished conception of the world for the next
philosophical congress, the "surrealist" hero throwing himself into a trance and plunging into the abyss
of dreams, the disciple of M. Gide viewing himself with
gloomy enthusiasm in the mirror of his freedom: all
those unhappy people are looking for their personalities;
and, contrary to the Gospel promise, they knock and no
man opens to them, they seek and they do not find.

See with what religious pomp the modern world
has proclaimed the sacred rights of the individual, and
what a price it has paid for that proclamation. Yet
was there ever a time when the individual was more
completely ruled by the great anonymous powers of the
State, of Money, of Opinion? What then is the mystery?

There is no mystery in it. It is simply that the
modern world confounds two things which ancient
wisdom had distinguished. It confounds *individuality*
and *personality*.

What does Christian philosophy tell us? It tells
us that the *person* is "a complete individual substance,

---

by the half-political, half-ecclesiastical character which it took on under
pressure from the State, that it had this primary effect so far as visible
institutions were concerned, is quite a different question and does
not affect our conclusions in any way. (*See* note 34.)

intellectual in nature and master of its actions," *sui juris, autonomous,* in the authentic sense of the word. And so the word *person* is reserved for substances which possess that divine thing, the spirit, and are in consequence, each by itself, a world above the whole bodily order, a spiritual and moral world which, strictly speaking, is not *a part* of this universe, and whose secret is hidden even from the natural perception of the angels. The word *person* is reserved for substances which, choosing their end, are capable of themselves deciding on the means, and of introducing series of new events into the universe by their liberty; for substances which can say after their kind, *fiat,* and it is so. And what makes their dignity, what makes their personality, is just exactly the subsistence of the spiritual and immortal soul and its supreme independence in regard to all fleeting imagery and all the machinery of sensible phenomena. And St. Thomas teaches that the word person signifies the noblest and highest thing in all nature: "Persona significat id quod est perfectissimum in tota natura."*

The word *individual,* on the contrary, is common to man and beast, to plant, microbe, and atom. And, whilst personality rests on the subsistence of the human soul (a subsistence independent of the body and communicated to the body which is sustained in being by the very subsistence of the soul), Thomist philosophy tells us that individuality as such is based on the peculiar needs of matter, *the principle of individuation* because it is the principle of division, because it requires to occupy a position and have a quantity, by which that which is *here* will differ from what is

* *Summa Theol.,* I, 29, 3. Cf. Cajetan's Commentary.

there. So that in so far as we are individuals we are only a fragment of matter, a part of this universe, distinct, no doubt, but a part, a point of that immense network of forces and influences, physical and cosmic, vegetative and animal, ethnic, atavistic, hereditary, economic and historic, to whose laws we are subject. As individuals, we are subject to the stars. As persons, we rule them.

9. What is modern individualism? A misunderstanding, a blunder; the exaltation of individuality camouflaged as personality, and the corresponding degradation of true personality.

In the social order, the modern city sacrifices the *person* to the *individual*; it gives universal suffrage, equal rights, liberty of opinion, to the *individual*, and delivers the *person*, isolated, naked, with no social framework to support and protect it, to all the devouring powers which threaten the soul's life, to the pitiless actions and reactions of conflicting interests and appetites, to the infinite demands of matter to manufacture and use. To all the greeds and all the wounds which every man has by nature, it adds incessant sensual stimuli, and the countless horde of all kinds of errors, sparkling and sharpened, to which it gives free circulation in the sky of intelligence. And it says to each of the poor children of men set in the midst of this turmoil: "You are a free individual; defend yourself, save yourself, all by yourself." It is a homicidal civilization.

Moreover, if a State is to be built out of this dust of individuals, then—and most logically, as the individual as such is, as I have said, only a part—the individual will be completely annexed to the social whole, will no

longer exist except for the city, and we shall see individualism culminate quite naturally in the monarchic
tyranny of a Hobbes, the democratic tyranny of a
Rousseau or the tyranny of the "Providence-State"
and the "God-State" of a Hegel and his disciples.

On the contrary, according to the principles of
St. Thomas, it is because he is first an individual
of a species that man, having need of the help of his
fellows to perfect his specific activity, is consequently
an *individual* of the city, a member of society. And
on this count he is subordinated to the good of his
city as to the good of the whole, the common good
which as such is more *divine* and therefore better
deserving the love of each than his very own life.[27]
But if it is a question of the destiny which belongs to
a man as a *person*, the relation is inverse, and it is
the human city which is subordinate to his destiny.
If every human person is made directly, as to his
first and proper good, for God, Who is his ultimate
end[28] and "the distinct and common good" of the
entire universe, he ought not therefore, on this
count, in accordance with his law of charity, to prefer
anything to himself save God.[29] So much so that
according as personality is realised in any being,
to that extent does it become an independent whole
and not a part (whatever be its ties on other grounds).
Thus the individual in each one of us, taken as an
individual member of the city, exists for his city, and
ought at need to sacrifice his life for it, as for instance
in a just war. But taken as a person whose destiny
is God, the city exists for him, to wit, for the advance-
ment of the moral and spiritual life and the heaping
up of divine goods; for that is the very end of

AETHERNA IPSE SVAE MENTIS SIMVLACHRA LVTHERVS
EXPRIMIT·AT VVLTVS CERA LVCAE OCCIDVOS

·M·D·X·X·

LUTHER IN 1520

From an engraving by LUCAS CRANACH (Fr. Lippmann, *Lucas Cranach,
Sammlung von Nachbildungen seiner vorzüglichsten Holzschnitte und seiner
Stiche*, 1895, n° 61)

LUTHER IN 1526

Painting by LUCAS CRANACH (Berlin, Kauffmann collection ; Ed. Flechsig, *Tafelbilder Lucas Cranachs*, 1900, nᵒ 85)

personality; and it is only by virtue of this that the city has its common good. Thus Christianity maintains and reinforces the moral framework and the hierarchies of the city, it has not denounced slavery[30] as of itself contrary to the natural law. But it calls slave and master alike to the same supernatural destiny and the same communion of saints. It makes every soul in a state of grace the dwelling of the living God; it teaches us that unjust laws are no laws, and that the Prince's command must be disobeyed when it is contrary to God's command. It bases law and juridical relations not on the free will of individuals, but on justice towards persons. Let us say that the Christian City is as fundamentally *anti-individualist* as it is fundamentally *personalist*.

This distinction between the individual and the person when applied to the relations between man and the city, contains, in the realm of metaphysical principles, the solution of many social problems. If, on the one hand,—and this explains the very essence of political life,—if the common good of the city is quite different from the simple aggregate of the benefits pertaining to each individual,[31] it is also different from the good pertaining to the whole, taken by itself; it is, so to speak, a *good common to the whole and the parts*, and it must in consequence admit of redistribution to the latter, considered no longer merely as parts, but as things and as persons. On the other hand,—and this concerns the end of political life,— if the earthly and temporal perfection of the rational animal has its realization in the city, in itself better than the individual, yet the city is essentially bound to ensure that its members have the conditions of a sound moral life, a properly human life, and bound to pursue the temporal good which is its immediate object only with respect for its essential subordination to the spiritual and eternal good to which every human person is ordered.* And since this spiritual and eternal good is in fact, by the Creator's grace, not the simple end of natural religion, but an essentially supernatural end—to enter by vision into the very joy of God—the human city fails in justice and sins against itself and its members if, when the truth is sufficiently proposed to it, it refuses to recognize Him Who is the Way of beatitude.[32]

10. In the spiritual order the distinction between individuality and personality is no less necessary. Fr. Garrigou-Lagrange has shown its bearing admirably: "Man will be fully a person, a *per se subsistens* and a *per se operans*, only in so far as the life of reason and liberty dominates that of the senses and passions in him; otherwise he will remain like the animal, a simple *individual*, the slave of events and circumstances, always led by something else, incapable of guiding himself; he will be only a part, without being able to aspire to be a whole. . . . "

"To develop one's *individuality* is to live the egoistical life of the passions, to make oneself the centre of everything, and end finally by being the slave of a thousand passing goods which bring us a wretched momentary joy."

"*Personality*, on the contrary, increases as the soul rises above the sensible world and by intelligence and will binds itself more closely to what makes the life of the spirit."

* Cf. *Summa Theol.* II–II, 83, b; in *Ethic Nicom.* I lect. 1.

"The philosophers have caught sight of it, but the saints especially have understood, that the full development of our poor personality consists in losing it in some way in that of God, Who alone possesses personality in the perfect sense of the word, for He alone is absolutely independent in His being and action."*

The personality of the wise is still very precarious and mingled! How much poor plaster there is on the stoic's austere mask. The privileges of personality,—the pure life of intelligence and liberty, the pure agility of the spirit, which is self-sufficient for action as for being,—are so deeply buried in our case in the matter of our fleshly individuality that we can only free them by being ready to fall to earth and die there in order to bear divine fruit, and we shall only know our true face if we receive the white stone on which God has written our new name. Truly perfect personality is only found in saints.

The saints have acquired in a sense, have received by grace, what God possesses by nature: independence of all created things, not only in regard to bodies but even in regard to intelligences. "The saints have their dominion, their glory, their victory, their brilliance, and have no need of carnal or intellectual dignities with which they have no relation, for they add nothing to them and take nothing from them; they are seen by God and the angels, not by bodies or curious minds. God suffices them."†

But did the saints set out to "develop their person ality"? They found it without seeking, because they

* R. Garrigou-Lagrange: *Le Sens commun*, 2nd ed. (Nouvelle Librairie Nationale), pp. 332–333.
† Pascal: *Pensées* (Brunschvicg, 793).

did not seek it, but God alone. They understood that their person, just in so far as it was person, in so far as it was free, was complete dependence on God, and that the inner control over our acts, which we cannot resign before man or angel, they must deliver into the hands of God, by Whose Spirit they must be moved in order to be His sons. "They understood that God must become for them another self, closer to them than their own selves, that God was more themselves than themselves, because He is eminently selfhood"; then they "sought to make themselves something of God, *quid Dei.*" *I am fastened to the cross with Christ. Now I live, yet not I, but it is Christ Who liveth in me.* Although in the order of Being they keep a self distinct from God's, "in the order of operation, of knowledge and love, they have, so to say, substituted the divine Self for their own,"*renouncing all personality or independence in regard to God, understanding that the first-born among them, their eternal model, had no human personality, but the divine Personality of the Word in Whom His human nature subsisted.

Such is the secret of our life as men which the poor modern world does not know: we gain our soul only if we lose it; a total death is needed before we can find ourselves. And when we are utterly stripped, lost, torn out of ourselves, then all is ours who are Christ's, and Christ Himself and God Himself is our good.

11. Luther's history, like that of Jean-Jacques, is a wonderful illustration of this doctrine. He did not free human personality, he led it astray. What he did free was the material individuality which we have just defined, the animal man. Cannot we see

* Garrigou-Lagrange: loc. cit., pp. 334–335.

it in his own life? As he gets older, his energy becomes less and less a soul's energy, and more and more the energy of a temperament. Driven by great desires and vehement longings which fed on instinct and feeling, not on intelligence; possessed by the passions, loosing the tempest around him, breaking every obstacle and all "external" discipline; but having within him a heart full of contradictions and discordant cries; seeing life, before Nietzsche, as essentially *tragic*,[33] Luther is the very type of modern[34] individualism (the prototype of modern times, Fichte calls him). But in reality his personality is disunited, ruined. There is much weakness of soul behind all his bluster.

It is significant that to free the human being he began by breaking the vows of religion; and the "joyful tidings," as Harnack calls it, which he announced to Christendom, at once spread an epidemic of despair over Germany.[35] German Protestants would have us recognize the *greatness* of Luther. Material greatness, quantitative greatness, animal greatness, yes, we will grant that, and, if you will, admire it; but truly human greatness, no. The confusion between these two kinds of greatness, or energy, between the individual and the person, is at the heart of Germanism, and it shows us why Germans conceive personality as a hurricane, a buffalo, or an elephant. It explains too why we see the old spring of the spirit of Luther gush out in all the great inspirers of Protestant Germany such as Lessing and Fichte. Fichte calls Luther the German *par excellence*, and that is true in so far as the Reformation succeeded in separating Germany from Catholicism.

Happy the nation whose supreme incarnation of her own genius is not a mere individuality of flesh but a personality radiant with the Spirit of God! If we want to set against Luther's egocentrism an example of true personality, let us think of that miracle of simplicity and uprightness, of candour and wisdom, of humility and magnanimity, of loss of self in God,— Joan of Arc.

§ IV. INTELLIGENCE AND WILL

12. Luther has another striking characteristic. He is a man wholly and systematically ruled by his affective and appetitive faculties; he is a Man of Will only, characterized chiefly by power in action. All historians insist upon his stark energy; Carlyle calls him *a Christian Odin, a very Thor.*

Certainly the will considered in its most peculiarly human characteristics is not here in question, that will which is more living as it roots itself more deeply in the spirituality of the intelligence. We are talking about the will in general, about what the ancients called in general the Appetite, the concupiscible appetite, and especially the irascible appetite.

It was said of him, "His words are half battles." When he is let loose, nothing can stop him. We know the magnificent violence of his challenges. "I should go to Worms were there as many devils there as tiles on the roofs." ·"I have seen and challenged innumerable devils. Duke George is not equal to a devil. If I had occasion to go to Leipzig, I should enter Leipzig on my horse, if it rained Dukes George nine days running."

With his extraordinary power of imagination and flow of words he must have been a fascinating talker, a truculent orator, doubtless often coarse and base, but irresistible. Bossuet very rightly remarked, "There was strength in his genius, vehemence in his speech, a lively and impetuous eloquence which carried crowds off their feet and enchanted them; extraordinary boldness when he found himself supported and applauded, together with an air of authority which made his disciples tremble before him, so that they dared not contradict him in anything big or little."* At the same time he was exceptionally endowed with that richly orchestrated sensibility in which the deep symphony of unconscious powers vibrates, and which makes the poetic and glowing charm of the *Gemüth*. We have a host of his touches of familiarity, good-fellowship, and kindness. Like Jean-Jacques, and no doubt more than Jean-Jacques, he was gifted by nature with a strong religious disposition: he prayed at length and liked to pray aloud, with a great flow of words which was the wonder of men; he was deeply moved at the sight of the harvest, the blue sky, a little bird which he watched in his garden. He wept over a violet found in the snow which he could not revive. Obsessed by a deep melancholy, no doubt the greatest and most human thing in him—by that melancholy of Saul which is so terrible to see because, if we did not know that Saul's eternal destiny, like Luther's, is reserved for the inscrutable judgement of God, we should be tempted to see in it the melancholy of those for whom it would have been

* *Hist. des Var.* I, 6.

better had they never been born,—that man who
unloosed the Revolution on the world was soothed
by music and took comfort in playing the flute. He
tells us that the devils fled from his flute.

All that comes from the same cause: the absolute
predominance of Feeling and Appetite. If the force
of instinct and the power of feeling is still ruled by
the spirit, then it provided the human being with
incomparable material and emotional wealth, and
these very things are used for the life of the spirit.
On this score there is already a certain romanticism,
if you like, in such as Suso, but in a conception of
life which remains fundamentally rational, ordered,
Catholic. With Luther it is otherwise; the will has
the primacy, truly and absolutely; it is the very
conception of life that is affected. We can say that he
is the first great Romantic.

13. That attitude of soul would naturally go with a
profound anti-intellectualism, which was besides
helped by the Occamist and nominalist training in
philosophy which Luther received. Let me quote
here a few characteristic passages. Let us first hear
him speak of Aristotle and St. Thomas.

"Aristotle is the godless bulwark of the papists.
He is to theology what darkness is to light. His
ethics is the worst enemy of grace."* He is a "rank
philosopher,"† an "urchin who must be put in the
pig-sty or donkey's stable,"‡ "a shameless slanderer,
a comedian, the most artful corrupter of minds. If
he had not lived in flesh and bones, I should not

* Cf. Ueberweg: *Grundriss der Geschichte der Philosophie*, III, 1914,
pp. 30, 32.
† Weim., IX, 43, 5, (1510–1511).
‡ Weim., VII, 282, 15–16 (1521).

IN SILENTIO FORTITVDO   ET SPE ERIT VESTRA.

LUTHER IN 1532
From the school of CRANACH (Munich)

LUTHER DEAD
By LUCAS FORTNAGEL (Leipzig, University Library)

scruple to take him for a devil."* As for St. Thomas,
"he never understood a chapter of the Gospel or
Aristotle."† Luther, "as he is fully entitled to do,
that is, with the liberty of a Christian, rejects and
abjures him."‡ "In short, it is impossible to reform
he Church if Scholastic theology and philosophy
are not torn out by the roots with Canon Law."§

"The Sorbonne, that mother of all errors," he
says in 1539, "has defined, as badly as could be, that
if a thing is true, it is true for philosophy and theology;
it is godless in it to have condemned those who hold
the contrary."‖ So too the faculty of Paris is "the
damned synagogue of the devil, the most abominable
intellectual prostitute under the sun, the true gate
of hell, etc."** The theologians of Louvain fare
no better; they are "coarse donkeys, cursed sows,
bellies of blasphemers, epicurean swine, heretics
and idolators, putrid puddles, the cursed broth of
hell."††

Has he a grudge against any particular system?
No. He is attacking philosophy itself. "Barking
against philosophy is a homage he thinks to give
to God . . . One should learn philosophy only as
one learns witchcraft, that is to destroy it; as one
finds out about errors, in order to refute them."‡‡

From him Carlstadt, as early as 1518, borrowed

---

* Letter to Lange, 8th February, 1516, de Wette, I, 15–16.
† Enders, I, 350, 25–30 (14th January, 1519); I, 173–174, 50–57
(24th March, 1518).
‡ Weim., I, 647, 33–34 (1518).
§ De Wette, I, 64, p. 108 (1518).
‖ *Disputationen*, 487, theses 4 and 5.
** Walch: *Luthers Werke*, XI, 5; XVIII, 1142; XIX, 1403.
†† Cf. Hofler: *Papst Adrian VI*, Wien, 1880, p. 41.
‡‡ Commentary on the Epistle to the Romans, fol. (1516).
Ficker, II, 198.

that fine thought, that "logic is nowhere necessary
in theology because Christ does not need human
inventions."* What? Dare to tie down a free
Christian like Dr. Luther to the principle of contradiction? Argument was never anything for him
but a boxing-match, in which he was past master,
and where the thing was to knock out his opponent
by any means. "When I care to start writing," he
said cynically to Philip of Hesse, "I shall be able to
get out of the difficulty easily and leave your Grace
to stick in the mud."† Finally, the Reformer declares
war not only on philosophy, but essentially on reason.
Reason has an exclusively pragmatic value, it is for
use in earthly life. God has given it to us only "to
govern on earth, that is to say that it has power
to legislate and order everything regarding this life,
like drinking, eating, and clothes, as well as what
concerns external discipline and a respectable life."‡
But in spiritual things it is not only "blind and dark,"§
it is truly "the whore of the devil. It can only
blaspheme and dishonour everything God has said
or done."‖ "The Anabaptists say that reason is a
torch. . . . Does reason shed light? Yes, like that
which filth would shed if it were set in a lantern."**

* Carlstadt to Spalatin, 5th February, 1518; Enders, I, 147, 105.
† De Wette, VI, 276. "As a polemic writer and author of theo-
logical works and especially as a popular controversial writer," says
Döllinger, "Luther joined to an indisputable talent for oratory and
dialectic a *lack of conscience* rarely met with in these matters in so high
a degree." It is well known that he called the Epistle of St. James
an "epistle of straw," because it contradicted his doctrine.
‡ Erl., 49, 229 (1538).
§ Ibid., 47, 728, 599 (1537–1540); 51, 400–401 (1523).
‖ Ibid., 29, 241 (1524–1525). He also writes "*Rationem atrocissimum
Dei hostem,*" in *Galat,* 1535, Weim XL, P.L., 363, 25.
** Cf. A. Baudrillart: *L'Eglise Catholique, la Renaissance et le protestant-
isme,* Paris, 1905, pp. 322-323.

And in the last sermon preached at Wittenberg, towards the end of his life: "Reason is the devil's greatest whore; by nature and manner of being she is a noxious whore; she is a prostitute, the devil's appointed whore; whore eaten by scab and leprosy who ought to be trodden under foot and destroyed, she and her wisdom . . . Throw dung in her face to make her ugly. She is, and she ought to be, drowned in baptism . . . She would deserve, the wretch, to be banished to the filthiest place in the house, to the closets." [36]

Luther's contempt for reason is, moreover, in harmony with his general doctrine about human nature and original sin. According to Luther, sin has vitiated the very essence of our nature, and this evil is final; grace and baptism cover over, but do not efface, original sin. So that the most that reason could be granted would be a wholly practical part in life and human business. But it is incapable of knowing first truths; and all speculative knowledge, all metaphysics is a snare: "omnes scientiae speculativae non sunt verae . . . scientiae, sed errores,"—and the use of reason in matters of faith, the claim to establish a coherent science of dogma and of the revealed deposit by reasoning and the use of philosophy, in short, theology, as the scholastics understood it, is an abominable scandal. In a word, this corrupted Christian takes with gross liberalism and in absolutely opposite sense the passages in which spiritual writers speak of the annihilation of the natural faculties, debases the thoughts of Tauler and the German mystics as well as the texts of St. Paul and the Gospel, and declares that faith is *against* reason. "Reason is contrary to faith,"* he wrote in 1536. And a little later: "Reason is directly opposed to faith, and one ought to let it be; in believers it should be killed and buried."†

I have quoted these passages because it is instructive to discern in the beginning, in its authentic tone and quality, the false anti-intellectualist mysticism which was to poison so many minds in more subtle and less candid guises in the nineteenth century. Luther in a word, brought a deliverance and an immense relief to humanity two hundred and thirty years before Jean-Jacques. He delivered man from the intelligence, from that wearisome and besetting compulsion to think always and think logically. Yet this liberation has constantly to be begun again. For, as he wrote in his commentary on the Epistle to the Galatians, "Alas, in this life reason is never completely destroyed."‡

. . . . .

14. We know well the problem Luther sets before us here; it is classical, it is of to-day, we are soaked in it. It is the problem of intellectualism and voluntarism. Luther is at the source of modern voluntarism. To prove this in detail, we should have to stress the

---

* *Disputationen,* ed. Drews, p. 42. "It is impossible to harmonize faith and reason." (Erl., 44, 158—[1537-1540].)

† Erl., 44, 156-157 (1537-1540). And again: "You must abandon your reason, know nothing of it, annihilate it completely or you will never enter heaven." (Ibid.) "You must leave reason to itself, for it is the born enemy of faith . . . There is nothing so contrary to faith as law and reason. You must conquer them if you would reach beatitude." *Tischreden,* Weim., VI (No. 6718), 143, 25-26, 32-35.

‡ *In Galat.,* (1535). Weim., XL. P.I., 364, 18-20.

consequences of the anti-intellectualist pessimism of which I have just spoken. As reason is banished to the foulest place in the house, if not killed and buried, the other spiritual faculty, the will, must be correspondingly exalted in practice if not in theory, for the brute pure and simple will never be an ideal for man. And so in Luther the swollen consciousness of the self is essentially a consciousness of will, of *realisation of freedom*, as German philosophy said later on. We should have to stress too his egocentrism, and show how the self is the centre for him, not, certainly, as in Kant, from a claim of the human intelligence to be the measure of intelligible things, but from the claim of the individual will, cut off from the universal body of the Church, to stand solitary and naked before God and Christ in order to ensure its justification and salvation by its trust.

It will be enough for me to show how the mysticism of the self and of the will is brought in by Luther. His teaching of the nothingness of works does not proceed from a Quietist error. Far from exaggerating the primacy which Catholic theology grants to contemplation, he abhors the contemplative life, and in his doctrine, as union with God by charity is quite impossible, religion tends in fact to be reduced to the service of our neighbour.[37] In short, actions and works are of no avail for salvation, and in this regard they are bad and corrupt. But they are good, devilish good (it is the right word here), for the present life. And as they can no longer be ordered to God, to what could they be ordered except to the realization of the human will? Rousseau dreams, but Luther

acts. He does not say, like Jean-Jacques: I cannot
resist my inclinations, but I am not wicked; I am good
in Your sight, O my God, I am essentially good.
He says: Adam's sin has corrupted me in my essence,
I am unclean, I sin greatly, but I trust in You, O my
God, and You take me and save me just as I am,
covering me with your Son's cloak. This is what he
himself says:

Have we sinned? "Jesus Christ stoops," says
Luther, "and lets the sinner *jump* on His back and
so saves him from death and the gaoler."* That is
what Christ is for. "What a consolation for pious
souls to put Him on like this and wrap Him in my sins,
your sins, the sins of the whole universe, and consider
Him thus bearing all our sins."† "When you see
that your sins cleave to Him, then you will be safe
from sin, death, and hell.‡ Christianity is nothing
but a continual exercise in *feeling that you have no sin
although you sin*, but that your sins are thrown on
Christ.§ It is enough to know the Lamb who bears
the sins of the world; sin cannot detach us from Him,
were we to commit a thousand fornications a day
or as many murders.[38] Is not that good news if,
when someone is full of sins, the Gospel comes and
tells him: Have confidence and believe and henceforth your sins are remitted? Once this stop is pulled
out, the sins are forgiven; there is nothing more to
wait for."|| From the moment when you acknowledge
that Christ bears your sins, He becomes the sinner

* Erl., 18, 58 (1537).
† *In Galat.* (1535) Weim., XL. P.I., 436, 24–26.
‡ Opp. exeg. lat., XXIII, 141; Weim., XXV, 330, 35, (1532–1534).
§ Ibid., 142; Weim., 131, 7.
|| Erl., 18, 260 (1522).

in your stead.* "And, as for you, you become the
beloved child and everything happens of itself, and
everything you do is good."† Come now! It is
practical to have a Christ. The Lord had said, "I
am in the midst of you as a servant, *ego in medio vestrum
sum sicut qui ministrat.*" "That is true, Saviour of
men. Serve me then, now, and cover me with
your coat." Behind Luther's appeals to the redeeming
Lamb, behind his outbursts of confidence and his
faith in the forgiveness of sins, there is a human
creature which raises its crest and manages very well
in the mud in which it is plunged by Adam's sin.
This creature will get straight in the world, it will
follow the will to acquire power, the imperialist instinct, the law of this world which is its own world, it
will work *its will* in the world. God will only be an ally,
a co-operator, a powerful partner. In the end, we
shall have the truly mad forms of voluntarism as
manifested in certain Anglo-Saxon pluralists, or in
M. Wincenty Lutoslawski, who cries out (so much does
he admire himself), *I cannot have been created*, and regards God as simply a power allied to and associated
with his own will. "We have almost the same object,
and consequently many enemies in common."

We are therefore fully justified in looking to Luther
for the origin of these two great ideas, which seem
inseparable in the history of philosophy: the idea of
radical evil, which passed into German philosophy
with Boehme, with Kant himself, with Schelling, with
Schopenhauer, and the idea of the *primacy of the will*,

* Weim., IX, 419, 36. Cf. Weim., (*in Galat.*), II, 504, 9 (1519).
"Peccata sua (credentis) jam non sua, sed Christi sunt." Weim.,
(*in Psalm*) V, 608 (1521), (*in Galat.* 1535), XL, P.I., 300-308, etc.
† Weim., XII, 559, 6-12 (1523).

which imposed itself on that same philosophy, particularly with Kant, Fichte, Schopenhauer,—as if Pessimism and Voluntarism were from a metaphysical standpoint the two complementary aspects of one same thought.

On another side, a whole wide current of modern thought,—this time French, rather,—which took rise with the Renaissance and Descartes, not with Luther, went in the opposite and not less erroneous direction to rationalism and optimism with Malebranche, Leibniz, the philosophy of illumination. Jean-Jacques, who was not embarrassed by metaphysics, found means to combine optimism and anti-intellectualism; but intelligence and will have never succeeded in being reconciled in modern philosophy, and the conflict of these two spiritual faculties cruelly rends the minds of men of this age.

15. The solution of the problem, as the ancients well knew, concerns all human life. That is why they kept their most subtle metaphysical elucidations for it. In the hope that there may be some courageous reader ready to bear with two or three rather technical pages, I will try in a short synthesis to sum up St. Thomas's teaching on this question.*

The intelligence, absolutely speaking, in itself and in the order of pure metaphysical hierarchies, is nobler and higher than the will: "intellectus est altior et nobilior voluntate." The reason is, that as both immaterially regard Being and Good, but under different aspects, the object of the intelligence, which is the simple essence of the Good in its intelligible constitution and in its truth, is, as such and in its pure formal line, simpler and more abstract, more

---

* Cf. *Summa Theol.* I, 82, 3.

purified and more strained out (if I may so say), more
perfectly spiritual, than the object of the will, which is
the desirable Good itself, taken in its concrete existence
and not simply in its intelligible *reason*, its *logos*.

This is shown by the fact, that if our intelligence
must necessarily use the senses, yet in its movement
towards the intelligible it leaves images behind it
as far as possible, whilst our will naturally carries
with it, in its movement towards what it loves, the
affections of the sensitive appetite. For from the
intelligence come all order and ordination, and at
the beginning of the ways of God is the Word, and,
from the Word, in God, proceeds the Spirit of Love,
as, in us, willing proceeds from understanding. And
our beatitude will essentially consist in *seeing*,
possessing God in a deifying vision, in which the very
being of God will be one with our intelligence in the
order of knowledge, and the love and delight in the
will will only be the consequence of this. So that in
us, at the last, Intelligence will perfectly enjoy its
metaphysical primacy over Will.

Not only then is the intelligence absolute queen in
the order of speculative truths and pure knowledge
(in the sense that that knowledge is perfect only if it
fully abstracts from every subjective attraction so that
it may be left wholly and purely dominated by the
object), but, moreover, in the practical order right
action supposes right knowing, reason is the proximate rule of our action, and every interior act of
the soul which involves order and government belongs
to reason.

16. And yet, if we consider intelligence and will
not in themselves, but in relation to the things in

greater or less degree of perfection which they may reach, then the order of superiority can be reversed and the will become higher than the intellect. This is so because, as Aristotle finely says, "bonum et malum sunt in rebus, verum et falsum in mente"*: the will seeks its object as it is in itself, in its existence and its own mode of being, whereas the intelligence seeks its object as it is in the intelligence, under the mode of being which it has from the intelligence, drawing it in and consuming it so as immaterially to become it. Hence in relation to things higher than we, the will, which carries us into these things, is nobler than the intelligence which draws them into us. And if it is better to know than to love corporeal things, which are below the soul and which the intelligence spiritualizes that it may know them, it is better to love God than to know Him, especially as things are in this present life where we know Him only according to the multiplicity and materiality of our conceptions. That is why there is a wisdom of the Holy Spirit higher above philosophic wisdom than heaven above earth, in which God is known and tasted not by distinct ideas, but by the connaturality of love proceeding from the union procured by charity.

On another side, if in the practical order we consider not the universal truths which rule action, but the concrete use which we make of our action, then St. Thomas assigns such preponderance to the part the will plays that the moral Part of the Summa seems as wholly magnetized by Will as the metaphysical Part by Intelligence. More intellectualist than Scotus so far as knowledge is concerned, he is much less

* Met., VI, 4, 1027 b 25.

intellectualist in regard to action. It is on the will that the *use* of our activity and all our movements to our Last End depend, so that it is by the will and not by our intelligence that we are styled *good* or *bad*, purely and simply. It is the will which by its freedom, its commanding indifference in regard to every created good, makes of our soul a sealed heaven which God alone can move and only the eye of God and the priestly glance of Christ can pierce. Finally, on the will and its presupposed general rectitude depends the truth of the practical knowledge which rules it in each concrete and specific case; for as the intelligence has no direct object but the universal, the pure object of speculation, it cannot well judge of what is to be *done*, of the singular and contingent, except by ordering the right inclination of the will. The truth of the practical intellect, which consists in *guiding*, not in *knowing*, is understood not by conformity with the thing, "per conformitatem ad rem," but by conformity with the right appetite, "per conformitatem ad appetitum rectum"; whence it follows that in the order of acting and of knowledge of each separate thing that can be done, the will, as Cajetan says, bends the intelligence at its pleasure, and that the practical judgement and the command of the intelligence can only be permanently good if the appetite is thoroughly rectified by the moral virtues.

17. Finally, St. Thomas shows us two complementary but essentially different activities in every mind, each as exacting and voracious as the other; an activity wholly turned towards the being of the object, towards what is "other" as it is "other," and of itself only concerned with that, living only for it,—

the intelligence; and an activity wholly occupied
with the good of the subject or of the things with
which the subject is united, which of itself is concerned
only with this good, living only for it,—the Will. Each
is predominant in its order, the one absolutely and
for knowledge, the other relatively and for action. Woe
to humanity if one monopolizes all the nourishment
at the expense of the other! If humanity is purely
and exclusively volitional, it contemns truth and
beauty and becomes the sort of moralist and fetichist
monster of which a Rousseau, a Tolstoy, or a William
James give us some idea. If humanity is purely and
exclusively intellectual, it scorns its eternal interests;
and what does its own being matter to it? It gets
intoxicated with the show, it becomes a kind of
monster, metaphysician or æsthetic. And doubtless
the more strongly a man is drawn in one direction by
his gifts, the more difficulty he has in keeping his
balance; the *glorious danger* of genius is always a
terrifying risk. If, in Thomas Aquinas, an intelligence so strongly drawn by the joy of pure knowledge
grew wholly in the straight way of holiness, it needed
an extraordinary strength of the moral virtues to
ensure the rectitude of the will. . . .

This doctrine explains the opposing excesses of
absolute intellectualism and absolute moralism, and
at the same time it harmonizes in its loftiness all
the truth in Goethe's thought, or Spinoza's, Tolstoy's
or Rousseau's. The reason is that it respects—and
it alone respects—the nature and laws which belong
to the intelligence and the will, without turning the
movements of the appetite into confused *ideas* (with
rationalism), or the operations of the intelligence

into a deformation of the real (with the philosophies of feeling).

Especially does this doctrine explain a twofold observation of experience very noteworthy for its practical importance: on the one hand, it is observed that privation of truth, particularly of the great metaphysical and religious truths, normally brings with it in the average state of a civilization moral disorder and the ruin of wills and great catastrophes; and that morals are often more effectively reformed by preaching high speculative doctrines than by the most earnest, most healthy, most social exhortations. But, on the other hand, all else being equal, how can we fail to observe also that intellectual power and virtue do not always go together? Let it not be a scandal to us that so many generous and sensitive souls are so weak in judgement, and so many clear and learned intelligences are so weak in morality; that there are so many virtuous folk not clever enough, and so many clever people not virtuous at all. Once the great speculative truths which rule our action are taken as known, the rectitude of our practical judgement in what concerns the moral *use* of our own activity depends not on the perspicacity of our speculative reason and the depth of our knowledge, but on the rectification of our will in relation to our personal ends, which are our own principles of action. That rectification can be perfect in a man who has very poor judgement about the part authority plays in the State, or the validity of the syllogism in *darapti* or *baralipton*, or the purgation of the passions by tragedy —although all these are questions which in themselves must be regarded as of prime importance.

That is why St. Thomas teaches that the moral virtues can exist without the intellectual virtues such as wisdom, science, and art, although they cannot exist without an understanding of first principles and without prudence, which is besides connected with them; so that all virtuous people necessarily use their reason, *"usus rationis viget in omnibus virtuosis,"* but only *"quantum ad ea quae sunt agenda secundum virtutem,"** as to the things which are to be done in matters of morality. There may be solid virtues in visionaries and philistines. That is an appreciable consolation of philosophy which is grateful in times like ours.

Lastly, the Thomist doctrine of the intelligence and the will shows us why all philosophy based on the absolute superiority of will or feeling, that is, of a faculty occupied essentially and exclusively with what affects the subject, will tend naturally to subjectivism; why, at the same time, it will cause the will to fall from its own order and will pass inevitably into the service of the lower affective powers and the instinct, for the metaphysical nobility and the spirituality of the will come only from its being an appetite rooted in the intelligence; why finally, such a philosophy, if it captures a part of humanity, means for it a series of disasters, simply because it asks light and guidance from a power in itself blind. *In the beginning* was Action: the motto of which the Germanic Faust is so proud is written on the standard of death.

* *Sum. Theol.* I–II, 58, 4, ad 2.

§ THE PRINCIPAL IMMANENCE

18. If an error creeps into minds, it is always thanks to some truth which it twists. There must be some basic illusion at the heart of the Lutheran Reformation which we need to seek. For that, there is no method better than to question the reformed themselves.

What do they tell us? They tell us that the essence of the Reformation is to exalt the Spirit against Authority, the interior energy of man, master of his judgement, against dead ideas and lying conventions imposed from without. What Carlyle sees in Luther is "a man self-subsistent, true, original, *sincere*." "With spurious Popes," writes this naïve Hegelian, "with spurious Popes, and Believers having no private judgement,—quacks pretending to command over dupes,—what can you do? Misery and mischief only. . . . In all this wild revolutionary work, from Protestantism downwards, I see the blessedest result preparing itself: not abolition of Hero-worship, but rather what I would call a whole world of Heroes. If Hero means *sincere man*, why may not every one of us be a Hero?" Why, indeed, why are not all sincere readers of Carlyle, Heroes? Why does not the *sincerity* of a scoundrel make him a martyr? The passage which I have just quoted is a good abridgement of anglo-modern stupidity, but I keep only the signs we are needing at the moment: the great ideas which the Lutheran error turned into illusions, the ideas of *liberty, inwardness, spirit.*

Here we touch the heart of the *immanentist* error. It consists in believing that liberty, inwardness, spirit, lie essentially in opposition to what is not the self,

in a breach between what is *within* and what is *without.*
Consequently truth and life must be sought only
within the human subject; everything in us that
comes from what is not ourselves (from what is
"other,"), is a crime against the spirit and against
sincerity.* And thus everything *extrinsic* to us is the
destruction and death of our interior. And every
mean which common sense regards as uniting interior
and exterior and bringing them into communication
is in reality an "intermediary" which separates
them. So, for modern Protestant individualism, the
Church and the Sacraments separate us from God; so,
for modern philosophic subjectivism, sensation and
idea separate us from reality. I do not say that
Luther formulated such a principle, far from it.
On the contrary, he had personally an excessively
dogmatic and authoritative conception of life and had
nothing of the liberal about him. But I do say that
it was he who in practice introduced this principle
to modern thought in a very special and still wholly
theological form, by setting up Faith against Works,
the Gospel against the Law, and by actually falsifying
that very faith to which alone he looked for salvation,
an heretical pseudo-faith which could not but come
down gradually to what it has become with many
Protestants of our days, a transport of distress and
trust towards the unknown from the deeps of the self.

What is remarkable here is, that this modern myth
of Immanence with its exaltation of the dignity of
the spirit is precisely based on a radical misunderstanding of the true nature of the spirit. To receive

* We have already dealt with this point in *Antimoderne* (Preface,
p. 24) but it is necessary to return to it here.

from others, from outside, is, indeed, in the world of
bodies, in the world of transitive action, pure submission, and is most certainly contrary to living spontaneity, since there we are dealing precisely with
lifeless things which, incapable of perfecting themselves,
serve only for the passage and transformation of
the energies of the universe. But to receive from
others in the spiritual world, that is certainly submission in the first place, but only as a presupposed
condition, and it is essentially action, to perfect
oneself interiorly and manifest the autonomy of what
is truly living. For the very quality of spiritual
things is that they are not confined within their
separate being and can increase intrinsically by
the being of what is not themselves. If the law of
the object, the law of being, imposes itself on the
intelligence, it is in order that the intelligence may
itself find vital completion in an action which is a
pure immaterial quality, and in which the very thing
which constitutes what is *"other"* becomes its own
perfection. And if the law of the Last End, the law of
the good, imposes itself on the will, it is that love may
make us one with the Author of all good, and that we
—by following His law, which has become ours,—may
still follow our deepest and most intimate attraction.
That is the mystery belonging to immanent activity,
perfect *interiorization*, by knowledge and love, of what
is "other", or of what comes from another than we.

In a still more transcendent order, before a yet
deeper mystery,—that of the creating Spirit's action
on created spirits,—Luther again isolates irremediably
what is *ourselves* from what is "other", ʾour spiritual
vessel from the surrounding ocean. He turns our

justice into a veneer under which we go on producing
our bad works, bad because "men's works, even
though they always seem beautiful and probably
good, are mortal sins," whilst God's works, were
they always ugly and apparently bad, are of eternal
merit.* "He does not even consider,"† says Bossuet,
"that men's good works are at the same time God's
works, since He produces them in us by His grace."[39]
This is the whole secret. For the immense God Who
is in the very heart of all things because He creates
them, and has dominion over Being itself, working
in each creature as befits the nature He gave it,
causes in spirits the action of spirits in the mode proper
to spirits, with all the spontaneity, inwardness, and
liberty which befit their nature. The absurd Lutheran
externalism may well pretend to give all to grace;
in reality, by regarding it as impossible that a work
of man should be also a work of God, it lays down the
principle of an unbridled naturalism which in a
little more than two centuries ruined everything in
Western thought before blossoming into contemporary immanentism. No longer is there any question
of the indwelling of the Divine Persons in our soul.
The soul is driven back into its solitude, it has become
impenetrable to everything but self.

19. The Reformer, and with him the whole modern
world, rises against two mysteries: the mystery of
the divine operations, and the mystery of immanent
activity and the capacity of spirits. Things perfectly
clear until then because they were accepted become

---

*Ap. Bossuet: *Hist. des Var.*, *I*, 9. (Prop. Heidls, an. 1518. Prop.
3, 4, 7, 11.)
  † Bossuet: Ibid.

obscure because they are denied. They can no longer keep anything of the things of the spirit but what is accidental and accessory, conditioned by the material and human. Intellectual *magisterium*, human or divine, Church and revealed dogma, even more radically, authority of objective being and the moral law, are finally no longer conceivable except as external and mechanical restraints forced on a nature which suffers them under compulsion. Now the lists are open.

Immediately after Luther, there is, for reasons of public safety and to avoid perishing of anarchy, a reaction of authority in Protestant Germany under the most tyrannously social form. What external compulsion is worse than to have princes legislating in spiritual matters and Churches separated from the Spirit of Christ? What discipline is more material and mechanical than Protestant scholasticism? What literalism is more oppressive than that of a dead theology and a "supernaturalism" based not on Primal Truth, but on the human reason of preachers paid by the State to interpret Scripture? What burden is heavier than their morality and that decalogue which terrified Luther and is terrible indeed, when the inward principle of grace no longer gives us strength and inclination to live in accordance with it?

But the spirit of Luther went on travelling underground, for new upheavals and new crises. And in such degree as the modern world and modern thought receive it, it gnaws them without respite and, because every spirit is stronger than matter, it swallows up, one after the other, all material prohibitions which restrain it for a time. The *essential* conflict of spirit and authority, of Gospel and Law, of subject and object, of intimate and transcendent, is a specifically Protestant conflict. It is meaningless in an order of things that takes account of spiritual realities, and modernism has tried in vain to carry it into the Catholic mind.

But see! By virtue of the principle of Immanence, since everything brought from outside is henceforth counted as oppression and force, it will, in the last analysis, be necessary to shut everything up in our spirit so that it may not have to receive anything from outside, and conclude all in man, including God Himself. Nature is itself dormant thought: in nature God is in process of becoming: and man will be the final stage of evolution at which that same nature will attain to self-consciousness.

The great "wild revolutionary work, from Protestantism downwards," thus prepares nonsense pure and simple as the "blessedest result."

It promises rest to the reason only in contradiction, it sets a universal war within us. It has inflamed everything, and healed nothing. It leaves us hopeless in face of the great problems, which Christ and His Doctors solved for redeemed humanity so long as it was faithful, problems which, nearly four centuries ago, once more began to rack the human heart like angelic instruments of torture.

DESCARTES

or

THE INCARNATION OF THE ANGEL

DESCARTES

or

THE INCARNATION OF THE ANGEL

Haec omnia tibi dabo. (Matth., iv, 9).
"From the age of Aristotle to the age of Descartes, I see a void of two thousand years. In that general torpor a man was needed to set the human species going again, to put new springs in the understanding: a man bold enough to upset, genius enough to rebuild; a man, etc." (Thomas: Éloge de Descartes.)

§ 1. THE CARTESIAN REVELATION

1. **I** OR my mind, he said. He produced his effect not, like Luther and Rousseau, by reproducing in souls the waves of his sensibility, the vast tumult of his heart, but by leading the mind astray, by captivating the reason with sines and clear ideas.

It would be little to our purpose to study the career and moral physiognomy of Descartes: the head superbly heavy and vehement, the low forehead, the discreet, stubborn, fanciful eye, the mouth proud and earthly; a strange life, secret and cunning, yet for all that strong and great from a single plan followed to the very end and a singularly clear and precocious understanding of the first condition of an intellectual amongst men, which is to flee them; the moment, short as a wing-beat, of that obscure dream by the German stove and of the call to philosophize until death for the renewal of humanity. What matters is his system; in it is his destiny formed.

53

I shall not undertake here an analytical examination of that system. I shall try to make its spiritual bearing clear. I address myself to readers familiar with Descartes in the confidence that they will recognize the points of doctrine to which I refer. Therefore I leave aside the human element which, in every philosopher and perhaps especially in this one, confuses the absolute of ideas and diminishes their pure force, and I want to give a bare, unadorned presentation, more direct than the original expression, not so much· of the philosophic work as of the *spirit* of Descartes.

2. Leon Bloy saw every commonplace of common speech as a sphinx crouching over the mystery of creation. It is an admirable way of experiencing ecstasy at every utterance of, say, our hall-porter, or member of Parliament. There is as much hidden wisdom in the commonplaces of philosophy, even of the history of philosophy. What do they tell us about Descartes?

As Luther discovered *the Human Person* and Jean-Jacques *Nature and Liberty*, Descartes discovered *Thought*. "He really revealed thought to itself," wrote M. Hamelin.* Let us not protest. That proposition is very true in the sense in which Hamelin took it. Let us say that Descartes unveiled the face of the monster which modern idealism adores under the name of Thought.

§ II. THE ANGEL AND REASON

3. Let us try to find the right names for things: the sin of Descartes is a sin of *angelism*. He turned Knowledge and Thought into a hopeless perplexity, an abyss of unrest, because he conceived human Thought after the type of angelic Thought. To sum it up in three words:

* O. Hamelin: *le Système de Descartes*, Paris, Alcan, 1911, p. 182.

What he saw in man's thought was *Independence of Things;* that is what he put into it, what he revealed to it about itself. Surely, you say, the crime is wholly mental, perpetuated in the third degree of abstraction; does it concern anyone but lunatics in long pedants' robes, those who have themselves bound in calf, as Councillor Joachim des Cartes said of his son? It has influenced some centuries of human history and havoc, of which the end is not in sight. Before indicating its consequences let us consider it in itself, and try to show its chief characteristics.

According to St. Thomas's teaching, the human intellect is the last of the spirits, and the most remote from the perfection of the divine Intelligence. As the zoöphyte bridges the gap between two kingdoms, so the rational animal is a transitional form between the corporeal world and the spiritual world. Above it, crowded like sea sand, rise in countless multitude the pure spirits in their hierarchies. These are *thinking substances* in the true sense of the word, pure subsistent forms, who certainly receive existence and *are* not existence, as God is, but they do not inform matter and are free from the vicissitudes of time, movement, generation and corruption, of all the divisions of space, all the weaknesses of individuation by *materia signata;* and each concentrates in himself more metaphysical stuff than the whole human race together. Each by itself is a specific type, and exhausts the perfection of its essence, and therefore they are borne, from the moment of their creation, to the complete fullness of their natural possibilities, incorrupt by definition. They raise above our heads a canopy of immensity, an abundance of stability and strength which, in comparison with us, is infinite. Transparent each to his own glance; each with full perception of his own substance *by* that substance, and at a single leap naturally knowing God also—by analogy, no doubt, but in what a mirror of splendour: their intellect, always in act with regard to its intelligible objects, does not derive its ideas from things, as does ours, but has them direct from God, Who infuses them into it when He creates it. And by these innate ideas, which are in it as a derivation from the divine Ideas, their intellect knows created things in the creative light itself, rule and measure of all that is. Infallible, then, and even impeccable in the natural order, considered apart from the supernatural end: autonomous and self-sufficing, so far as a creature can be self-sufficing: the life of the angels is an endless outflow of thought, knowledge, and will, without weariness or sleep. Piercing, in the perfect clearness of their intuitions, not, of course, the secrets of hearts nor the unfolding of future contingencies, but all essences and all laws, the whole substance of this universe; *knowing the power and actions of fire, water, air, the stars, the heavens, all other bodies, as distinctly as we know the different occupations of our workmen,* they are finally, without hands or machines, *as masters and possessors of nature,** and can play upon nature as on a guitar by modifying the movement of the atoms at their will. In all this we are speaking of the attributes of the angelic nature considered in itself, and, apart from its elevation to the supernatural order, as it subsists in fallen and faithful spirits alike. That is the model on which a son of Tourraine set out one day to reform the human mind.

* Cf. *Disc. de la Méth. VIe P.,* (A.-T., VI, 62.)

4. Consider the three great notes of angelic Knowledge—INTUITIVE, as to its mode, INNATE, as to its origin, INDEPENDENT OF THINGS, as to its nature. You find these three same notes again, transposed certainly, but not less fundamental and not less manifest, in human Knowledge according to Descartes.

5. Descartes's first effort, as we know, aims at freeing philosophy from the burden of discursive reasoning, at opposing to the laborious farrago of the School and its swarm of syllogisms raised one on another a ready, distinct, level science, a sheet of clearness. But see where that search for the simple actually leads. When our understanding apprehends, judges, and reasons, it is no longer tied down to three operations irreducibly distinct in nature. It has but one function: vision. A fixing of the pure and attentive intelligence on such or such object of thought, with well defined lines, with nothing of the implicit or virtual, grasped fully and wholly by absolutely original and primary vision and with a certitude grounded on itself alone—that is what Descartes calls intuition, "intuitus,"* and it is to that henceforth that everything in the cognizant understanding is reduced.

For Descartes makes the judgement, the operation of assenting, of interior conviction, no longer belong to the understanding, but to the will, which alone is active: it is a decision of the will, which comes to *agree* to an idea as a faithful representation of what is, or may be.

And after "intuition," he does indeed admit another operation, which is "deduction," the operation of reasoning; but that consists of nothing more than

* Cf. *Regulae ad directionem ingenii*, Reg. 3, A. T., t. X, 368; Reg. 10 (X, 419-425).

constructing new objects of apprehension by combining intuitions; a concession perforce to discursive reasoning but clumsy and contradictory, which destroys the unity belonging to reasoning and the continuity of logical movement and replaces it by a discontinuous succession of motionless glances.[40] To reason is no longer *to be led* by the principle to see the consequence, it is to *see* the principle and its connexion with the consequence *together*. Behind the banal attacks on the syllogism in the *Regulae*, we must see a tenacious zeal to reject that work of patient production of certitude which constitutes the life of the reason as such, and by which, considering one truth in the light of another, a new light is born and rises in us, in which what was virtual and hidden in the truth already known shines out clearly.

6. This logical denial is of peculiar importance. To lay hands on the syllogism is to lay hands on human nature. What Descartes really attacks, in his impatience of the servitude of discursive work is the potentiality of our intellect, that is to say, its specifically human weakness, what makes it a *reason*. So by curious chance the first move of rationalism is to disown reason, to do violence to its nature, to challenge the normal conditions of its activity. Behold it reconstructed after an intuitive type, stiff in the tinsel of pure intelligence and in a parcelling-out of comprehending immobilities.

The secret desire of the intelligence in search of a superhuman condition is to reduce all to simple perception—but this is a desire which only grace makes truly realizable, in the transluminous night of contemplation. Descartes, for his part, set himself to that from the first, and in the very work of the reason. He wanted to effect such a concentration of evidence that the whole train of conclusions might be grasped by simple intuition of the principle: that alone is worthy of Science! And as he could not manage that, he would despair and confess himself beaten by the evil Genius, did he not think that, in the initial certitudes of the *cogito* and the ontological proof, he had found an argument as ready and direct as simple intuitive perception. He would despair, did he not also think that by making the thought of God and the divine truthfulness coexistent and coextensive with the whole advance of knowledge, and by setting the philosopher in the ever-present light of the idea of God,[41] he could remedy the impossibility in which we are (and to which he will never submit), of having, at the actual moment when we make the inference, gathered up in one single and indivisible present (in which memory has nothing to do) the present—and compelling—evidence of all the previously established conclusions which serve us as premises.

What does this mean, but that the sole authentic and legitimate archetype of Knowledge is, for him, angelic Knowledge? The angel neither reasons, nor proceeds by reasoning: he has but one intellectual act, which is at once perceiving and judging: he sees consequences not successively from the principle, but immediately in the principle; he is not subject to the progressive actualization of knowledge which constitutes logical movement properly so called; if his thought travels, it is by intuitive leaps, from perfect act to perfect act, from intelligible fullness to intelligible fullness, according to the discontinuity of wholly spiritual time, which is not a succession of instants without duration, (like the time, also discontinuous, which Descartes

c

attributes to our world) but the permanence of a stable instant which lasts motionless so long as it does not give place to another motionless instant of contemplation. That is the ideal limit, the pure type of reason conceived in the manner of Descartes.

7. The angelic intellect is not made of faked-up intuitions, like the Cartesian understanding; it is genuinely intuitive. It is true that it is infallible, at least in the natural order, and that is so necessary a consequence that the fact of error is very troublesome to Cartesian optimism, the most difficult of humiliations to admit and the most difficult to explain.

How is it possible that I should be mistaken, I who am spirit? How can a substance whose whole nature is to think, think wrongly? It is so serious an anomaly that the author of things seems compromised by the scandal. I am mistaken only because I will have it so, my free will alone is to blame. And therefore human error is explained for Descartes in the same way as theologians explain angelic error; I mean, more precisely, than the Cartesian theory of error, so little consistent with his position, would only become coherent and logical if one brought to it, with suitable emendation, the case of the errors of fallen spirits. Precipitancy of judgement! When they err (which only happens to them when they are dealing with the supernatural order), they see in full light an object whose natural reality they completely apprehend, and they also see not less clearly the contingent and conjectural bond between that object and any other—for example, some future event—which remains dark to them. And when they impetuously extend their affirmation beyond what they see, and give their assent precipitately, I mean by deliberate inadvertence, to a thing which is not evident to them, it is because they are carried away by the malice of their will: *"sciens et volens non se detinet, sed judicat ultra quam potest."** Such, according to Descartes, is man when he affirms and judges beyond what he perceives clearly and distinctly, from a weakness of his free will, from an impetuosity for which his will is solely responsible, and that just in so far as it is free.[42] Due allowance being made, we cannot help remarking here a strange likeness between this psychology of error in the fallen Angel and the psychology of error in us according to Descartes.

In consequence of this angelist psychology the philosopher will demand such a criterion of certitude that to avoid error it shall be enough for us at every moment to survey the field of our representations with a true will not to be deceived. To look into ourselves, to separate the obscure from the clear, and the confused from the distinct, and agree only to the clear and distinct, so that it shall rest as much and as rightly with our will that we should not err in speculation as that we should not sin in action: that is the art of infallibility which the criterion of clear ideas should teach us.† Obviously such a science ought to be constructible—under ideal conditions, instantaneously —at the worst easily and quickly: the greater the speed, and the fewer the minds concerned with its construction, the better. Was not one enough for it?

---

* John of St. Thomas: *Curs. theol.*, q. 58, disp. 22, a. 4, n. xxii (Vivès, IV, p. 860).
† "To reach truth," said Malebranche, "it is enough to make oneself attentive to the clear ideas which each finds in himself." (*Rech. de la vérité*, I. 1.) Taine: *Ancien Régime*, III, 2 quotes this saying as characteristic of the classical spirit,—let us call it more exactly the Cartesian spirit.

If he were in a position to make all the experiments he needs, would not Descartes himself refound and complete the whole body of wisdom? He has no time to lose, he is a man in a hurry (like all moderns). If he can only snatch some tens of years from death, the great work on which the happiness and perfection of humanity depend will be done. In any case it will not need more than two or three centuries—this we now have the pleasure of verifying.

If Cartesianism showed itself so savage a ravager of the past in the intelligible order, it is because it began by disowning in the individual himself the essential intrinsic dependence of our present knowledge on our past, which makes our establishment in truth, humanly speaking, necessarily and of itself a strangely long and laborious thing. In a general manner, whether the poor effort of the individual or the common work of generations is in question, the Cartesian angel only submits to time as to an external compulsion, a force repugnant to his nature; he does not understand the essential function of time in bringing human cognition to maturity.

.   .   .   .   .

8. The ideas of the angel, as we have said, are innate: they do not come from objects, like our abstract ideas; they are infused into him, received at the beginning like a dowry of light. They are certainly accidents, really distinct from the angelic substance and its intellective power, and superadded gifts, but they are required as of right by the nature of the pure spirit.

From the fact that Descartes refuses to acknowledge the reality of accidents distinct from substance, his innatism remains bound in inextricable difficulties. Sometimes innate ideas are proximate dispositions to think this or that, yet still confused with the thinking nature itself, which puts in the latter, as it were, hidden preformations which already foreshadow the Leibnitzian virtualities. Sometimes the soul differs from its thoughts as extension from its shapes, and for Descartes, (who, by one of his frequent clumsinesses, here wrongly applies the scholastic notion of mode,)[43] that means that the act of thinking this or that is not an accidental but a substantial determination, a completion of the thinking substance in its very substantiality. As if an operation could be substantial elsewhere than in the Pure Act! He thus pictures mode as a substantial completion in the operative order. Spinoza took this bastard notion and made a pretty monster of it.

It remains—and this is what concerns us—that the Cartesian ideas come from God, like angelic ideas, not from objects. Thus the human soul is not only subsistent as the ancients taught, causing the body to exist with its own existence; it has, without the body, received direct from God all the operative perfection which can befit it. There is the destruction of the very reason of its union with the body, or rather, there is its inversion. For if the body and the senses are not the necessary means of the acquisition of its ideas for that soul, and consequently the instrument by which it rises to its own perfection, which is the life of the intelligence and the contemplation of truth, then, as the body must be for the soul and not the soul for the body, the body and senses can be there for nothing but to provide the soul—which needs only itself and God in

order to think,—with means for the practical subjuga-
tion of the earth and all material nature, and this
reduces the soul's good to the domination of the
physical universe. This universe, the whole of which
has not the value of one spirit, will make it pay dear
for this deordination. This angel is iron-gloved, and
extends its sovereign action over the corporeal world
by the innumerable arms of Machinery! Poor angel
turning the grindstone, enslaved to the law of matter,
and soon fainting under the terrible wheels of the
elemental machine which has got out of order.

9. But to come back to the Cartesian theory of
Knowledge. If our cognition is like an outflow of the
creative truth into our spirit, if wisdom, of which we
bear all the innate germs in the nature of our soul, is
a pure unfolding of our understanding, human science
must be *one*, with the oneness of the understanding;
there can be no specific diversity of sciences. And thus
there will be no specific diversity of knowledge ruling
the judgement, no varying degrees of certitude.[44]
Certainly it is so with the angel, for all his certitudes in
the natural order are unique in degree,—even the
degree of perfection of his own immateriality and his
innate knowledge. In Descartes the result is the most
radical levelling of the things of the spirit: one same
single type of certitude, rigid as Law, is imposed on
thought; everything which cannot be brought under it
must be rejected; absolute exclusion of everything that is
not mathematically evident, or deemed so. It is inhuman
cognition, because it would be superhuman! There is
the source not only of Descartes' proclamation of brutal
contempt for the humanities, for Greek and Latin: "It
is no more the duty of a sound man to know Greek or

DESCARTES
From the portrait by FRANZ HALS (Louvre)

Latin than to know Swiss or Low-Breton,"—for history, for erudition,* for all the huge realm of positive and moral studies which his successors later reduced to absurdity in the desire to make of them a "mathematics of the contingent"; but it is the principle and the origin of the deep *inhumanity* of our modern science.

Moreover, innatism, making of the intellect a power predetermined by nature to all the objects of its knowledge, does not allow that our understanding should be intrinsically determined and raised as by a grafting in it of the object to be known or the end to be attained, in order to produce a perfect work wherever it be, whether in the speculative or practical order. No more than with the angel in the natural order, are there elevating qualities or *habitus* in the Cartesian intellect.

Hamelin noticed rightly that one of the causes of the passion for method in the time of Descartes—at that time when modern man, the better to start his attack on the world, left the old supports of intellectual tradition—was the need to justify so much confidence by replacing these supports by a good insurance against error. To tell the truth, what the *guaranteed success* of the process and the recipe had to do duty for was not only the aids of the *via disciplinae*, but also and especially the interior vigour of the *habitus*. And thus common sense will do for everything.[45] The shop of clear ideas is the *Bon Marche* of wisdom. After Descartes, prices will go up again, and that fine universal facility will

---

* "Adam," Malebranche said, "did not know history and chronology in the earthly paradise. Why seek to know more than he?" We must not forget that men like Saumaise, Petau, Sirmond, du Cange, Mabillon, were the glory of French erudition in the seventeenth century, which people have sometimes tried to characterize completely by the Cartesian spirit.

give way to the most fearful complications. But it is always by method, or by methods, and no longer by the spiritual quality ennobling the intellect, that the austerity of knowledge will be measured. We see in our days the cheering effects of this materialization of science, and the astonishing intellectual beggary that an advance, admirable in itself, in technical special-ization and operative processes can bring about: for the flame remains feeble on which piles of green wood are flung.

.   .   .   .   .

10. The deepest quality of angelic cognition is not that it is intuitive or innate, but that it is independent of external objects. The ideas of pure spirits have no proportion with ours. As they are resolved in the very truth of God and not in the truth of external objects, these infused ideas are a created likeness, and as it were a refraction, in the angelic intellect of the divine ideas and the uncreated light where all is life. So that they represent things just in so far as things derive from the divine ideas, for the angels have thus received, at the first instant, the seal of likeness which made them full of wisdom and perfect in beauty—*tu signa-culum similitudinis, plenus sapientia et perfectus decore**—and God, as St. Augustine says, produced things intelligibly in the knowledge of spirits before producing them really in their own being.

Moreover, these ideas, unlike our abstract ideas, are universal not by the *object* which they present to the intelligence immediately, but only by the means which they constitute of reaching from the same point of view a multitude of natures and individuals distinctly

* Ezech., xxviii, 12.

apprehended even to their ultimate differences. Their universality is not the universality of representation due to the process of abstraction, but the universality of causation or activity belonging to the creative ideas, whence things descend into being, and of which the angel's ideas are a likeness cut to his measure. They are, John of St. Thomas tells us, like copies of models—but sparkling with spiritual vitality—like models imprinted on the angelic intellect, in which is figured the countless swarm of creatures flowing from the supreme art, as God sees it even before bringing it into existence: though doubtless not in the absolute unity of the divine vision, but distributed according to the capacity of created spirits, under certain great categories, by the unity of objects in their relation to such or such an end, and in the mode in which they proceed from their divine exemplars. And so, like the divine causality and the divine ideas, the ideas of the angel go down to existence itself: they directly touch the individual existence, comprehensively known by pure intelligences so far as it receives being and responds, in the concrete of matter then given, to its eternal archetype refracted in the pure spirit.

It is thus that the angelic cognition, depending solely on the knowledge of God, is independent of objects, from which it does not draw its ideas, and which are not its formal rule—independent, we may say, if at least we are talking of the lower world, in regard to its very objects of intellection, which it precedes, which it awaits, of which it is the measure, which it fully apprehends by the very efficacy of the creative knowledge, and to the intelligibility of which it has not to proportion the degree of immateriality of its ideas.

We see in what eminent sense the angel knows all the things of this lower world *a priori* and by their supreme causes, since he knows them by a participation in the very ideas which make them, since he knows the work of art—I mean all this universe—in what the artist tells him about his operative science, the very cause of being and all beauty.

11. Now look at the Cartesian understanding. Does not that also hang immediately on God, rising above and measuring all material nature without receiving anything from it? By one of those slips due to his resolve to go quickly in the work, Descartes applies to the certitudes of reason and science the classical solutions of the traditional teaching about the formal motive of faith: *veritas prima revelans*, the authority of God revealing. It is because God cannot lie that clear and distinct ideas deserve our assent, and he who does not know the divine truthfulness is strictly certain of nothing. If we could not lean on the guarantee of the truthfulness of the Creator, author of things and author of our mind, we could not *know* on trustworthy authority that there is a material world, or that there exist outside our thought things in conformity with our ideas, or even that these ideas deliver to us anything of the authentic, intelligible object or of the eternal truths, and do not deceive us even in what we conceive as most evident. That well shows that rational cognition is for Descartes a sort of *natural revelation*,* and that our ideas, like the infused species of the angel, have their immediate pattern in God, not in objects.

Yet, surely, unlike the angelic intellect, the Cartesian understanding reaches directly neither individuality

* Cf. Bordas-Demoulin: *Le Cartésianisme*, I, 29; Hamelin, op. cit., 233.

nor existence. Be undeceived. However ill or hastily Descartes may have expressed himself on general ideas,[46] it seems clear that in his eyes they are essentially incomplete notions—Spinoza later called them inadequate. Human science, if it is to be perfect, must reach singular essences by direct apprehension. A universal *means* of thinking, in the angelic fashion, all well and good! A universal *object* of thought, an abstract quiddity whose singular mode of realization we know only by a return to images, that is not worthy of the spirit to which all matter is subjected. Hardly indicated in Descartes, that disregard of nature and of the importance of the universal *in praedicando*—of the properly human universal—that sort of intellectualist nominalism developed fully with Leibnitz and Spinoza; with them it became one of the signs of the claim to be as the angels which characterizes absolute intellectualism, until, falling into English heads and rejoining the old sensationalist nominalism, it helped to ruin every sound notion of abstraction.

As to the perception of the existent as such, we may say that the transition to existence, the grasp of existence by the help of the intelligence alone and starting from pure ideas, forms just the crucial problem of the Cartesian philosophy. For as our ideas are no longer resolved (materially) in things by means of the senses, whose data have no longer anything but pragmatic and subjective value, existence and the placing of things outside nothingness is no longer conveyed to us at once by our fleshly contact with the world. We must arrive at being, we must rejoin it, or deduce it, or beget it, from an ideal principle set or discovered in the depths of thought. There is the impossible task to which, from Descartes to Hegel, the metaphysics of the moderns is condemned. Descartes kept the scholastic teaching that the perception of our human intelligences reaches directly only essences, and therefore cannot by itself cross the vast sky which separates the possible from existent reality. For him, meanwhile, pure thought must be self-sufficient, and the philosophizing intelligence cannot, even in the order of the *resolutio moralis*, essentially need to have recourse to the senses, which of themselves yield to us only modifications of our consciousness, appearances, uncertainty. Must one, then, renounce for ever any meeting with Being? No. There are privileged cases in which the pure intelligence suffices to reach it; it is so with the *cogito*, in which thought transparent to itself knows its own existence not by an empirical verification, but by an immediate grasp of its substantial ground in an act of intellection; it is so with the proof of God by the idea, in which thought has only to fix itself on the imprint of Perfection in it to read there openly Its real existence. It is a twofold intellectual revelation of existence in which alone human reason reaches its full spiritual measure, and behaves like the angel knowing himself and his author.

My thought exists, God exists. All flows from that. It is from God that the Cartesian science descends to things and deduces Physics. It is perfect science, science by causes, the only one proportioned to the philosopher's ambition. It also knows this universe *a priori* and according to the very order of creative reasons. (If it fails in the task, it will be to hand it over to the metaphysics of Spinoza.) Does it expect anything from the senses, for after all one does not

quite forget that one is human? The senses have only
an accidental part, in particular that of selecting
between the equally possible different ideal combin-
ations and of showing us which has actually been
realized.

Such, in its first manifestation, appears to us the
independence of the Cartesian reason in regard to
external objects; separation between the intelligence
and the senses by which the intelligence was in continuity with external objects, with the existent singular.
Contempt of the body in the work of science, refusal
of animal cognition which first binds us to creation,
refusal of that properly human condition of being able
to know only by the senses and the intellect together
what the angel knows by intellect alone. See that fine
science set out. Is it fairly sure of itself? It will go far.
But Kant is waiting for it at the turn of the road. If
the senses, he will say to it, only yield pure appearances to us and are not to our minds the vehicle of
what is, to reach being you would need, O presumptuous one, a supersensible intuition, even that enjoyed
by the pure spirits in whose image you have been
re-formed. But you have no such intuition in your
luggage. Ergo, you will never know that which is,
and all your *a priori* is only a phenomenal structure.

12. There is a second aspect, perhaps more specific,
of the independence of the Cartesian reason with
respect to things. This time it is less a question of
sensible things as such than of their intelligibility, and
therefore of the proper object of the intelligence.

For St. Thomas, and it is a logical consequence of
the abstractive nature of our intelligence, the sole
absolutely first object reached by it is Being in general,

and in that it resolves all its conceptions, learning at
the dictation of experience to make explicit the differences contained in it. Now it is most evident that
Being, which permeates all things, is hostile to no
reality; it welcomes them all, it is the Abraham's
bosom, if I may venture to call it so, in which rest all
the fauna of creation, all the forms which flow from
the Poetry of God, however noble and rare, poor or
luxuriant they may be. Hence it follows that an analysis
carried out in terms of Being, elaborating the concepts
of our science according to the requirements of reality,
docile to the analogy of transcendentals, following with
fidelity and obedience, with tenderness and devotion,
the outlines of that which is, will be able to penetrate
into things and put essences into intelligible communication without any injury to their originality,
their unity, their own secret. That is why although the
brain of a Thomist may be as limited and hard as every
human brain and very disproportioned to the wisdom
he defends, yet none the less he has the consolation of
telling himself that, considering the doctrine in itself,
if not the doctor, there is nothing in heaven and earth
which is not at home in his theology.

For Descartes, on the contrary, and it is a logical
consequences of his innatism, thought finds in itself a
plurality of ideas, ready made, irreducible, irresolvable,
each clear by itself, each the object of primary intuition,
intelligible elements to which everything that knowledge has to do with must be reduced. These are the
"simple natures" which are like atoms of obviousness
and intelligibility.[47]   As he suppressed the material
resolution of our concepts in external objects, Descartes
suppresses their formal resolution in Being.

Nor do the angels cut out their ideas from the common cloth of Being, but that is because they fully apprehend the whole reality of a section of creation by a single one of their comprehensive ideas. Whereas to replace resolution in being by reduction to simple natures—to thought, for things of the soul; to extension and motion for things of the body—can only produce incalculable mischief in an understanding which, however much it may dislike it, remains discursive, and whose whole work consists in advancing by composition of concepts.

What the Cartesian revolution introduces here is nothing less than a radical change in the very notion of intelligibility, and correlatively in the very type of scientific intellection and "explanation."

Unqualified in principle to comprehend the analogy of being and to use it, and so from the first closing to itself approach to divine things, the Cartesian analysis, cutting up and levelling down, can only break the internal unity of beings, destroy alike the originality and diversity of natures, and violently bring everything back to the univocal elements which it has been pleased to select as simple principles. Henceforth, to understand is to separate; to be intelligible is to be capable of mathematical reconstruction. To take a machine to pieces and put it together again, that is the high work of the intelligence. The mechanical explanation becomes the only conceivable type of scientific explanation.

Criterion of obviousness! There is nothing more equivocal and less loyal than the Cartesian clearness and distinctness. Let us clearly understand that Cartesian obviousness is wholly different from the obviousness designated by the ancients, and by the common usage of men, as the criterion of certitude. That obviousness is a property of Being, *fulgor objecti*, and it manifests itself to our mind in self-evident propositions known of themselves, first principles of our knowledge. It forces us to difficult elaborations in order to keep these principles faithfully, yet without in any way disregarding experience, in order to sin neither against reason nor against reality. The more it makes our science grow, the more it makes us perceive that Being is our measure and that there is nothing of which we know the whole. Finally, whether it is question of power, matter, contingency, of what is in itself least intelligible, or of the things of the spirit and of God—to a sovereign degree intelligible in themselves but to our intellect as the sun to an owl's eyes—it leads us to objects dark either in themselves or for us, and makes us issue out on mystery, mystery of imperfection or perfection. What does it matter? It is a luminous night, in which the necessities of thought trace for us a surer way than the orbits of the planets.

Cartesian obviousness, on the contrary, is a subjective obviousness, a quality of certain ideas, and it is not in the *propositions* regulating the progression of our certitudes, it is in *notional objects*, the term of the analysis of things, that it is manifested to our mind. There are *ideas* which are self-evident and perfectly penetrable by our thoughts. These ideas are the matter of science. All the others must be reduced to them or be eliminated. These are the things which lie open to the Cartesian angel. Far from the corporeal world concealing a residue of relative unintelligibility, it is perfectly clear to our human perception, being nothing but geometrical extension, perfectly subject to our spirit in cognition before being perfectly subject to it in practice. With this fatal meeting of pantheism and absolute intellectualism, we soon have, confronting an intelligence which imagines itself as in pure act of intellection, a universe which is imagined as in pure act of intelligibility. We really have all things forcibly adjusted to the level of human ideas, the treasures of experience squandered, creative art profaned, and the work which God made replaced by the inane world of rationalism.

To tell the truth, as our reason drifts and has no rule in it when separated from Being, clear ideas understood in Descartes' sense furnish no consistent criterion. Actually they are reduced to ideas which are easy or "easy to conceive"; and the Cartesian clearness is synonymous with facility. Ought not science, then, to be easy to man as it is to the angel? That is why Mathematics becomes the Queen of Sciences and the norm of all knowledge. Everywhere else, under cover of this pretended strictness, the arbitrary creeps in, following a law of irony which we see daily verified (of which German exegesis gives a good illustration in the nineteenth century). Bossuet says in a celebrated passage, "Under the pretext that we must not accept anything but what we understand clearly—which, within certain limits, is very true— everyone gives himself liberty to say, 'I understand this, and I do not understand that,' and on this sole basis they admit and reject whatever they like."* In practice, for truth measured by Being Cartesian

* Letter to the Marquis d'Allemans, 21st May, 1687 (Urbain et Levesque, III, 372–373).

obviousness could not but substitute facility in reasoning and tractability of ideas. The Philosophy of Illumination, lighting heaven with the candles of the Encyclopædia, will thus very naturally continue the philosophy of clear ideas.

Let us say that, in all that, the Cartesian understanding claims independence with respect to its object, with respect not only to things as the object of the senses, but to things as the object of science. Descartes is an out-and-out dogmatist, and from this point of view the very opposite of a subjectivist. But with him human science, drunk with mathematics, begins no longer to be measured by the object. For its constitution, its existence as a science, it no longer asks the object to impose its law upon it, it imposes on the object a measure and a rule which it thinks it finds in itself. Thus while the science of the Angel, although independent of external objects, does not deform the object which it reaches, because it reaches it by a likeness of the creative ideas, cause and measure of that object and of its being, the Cartesian science does violence to reality in order to reduce it to the predestined scale of "scientific" explanations. Thenceforward the human intelligence becomes the law-giver in speculative matters; it fashions its object. We may say that Cartesian reason practised Kantian *apriorism* before it was named (*in actu exercito*). Kant afterwards only had to observe that in good logic an understanding which fashions its objects without producing them in being can only have phenomena for its objects and not things in themselves. Cartesian dogmatism, after a long flight, will have become agnosticism when it falls to earth.

13. The Angel knows himself immediately by his substance, in a perfect intuition which yields him the ground of his being. His natural cognizance of God is consummated not only in his beholding external objects, but primarily and above all in beholding himself, in the most pure mirror of his own essence. His own essence is the first object of his intellection, and he is always in act of intellection of himself. Everything he knows, he knows by first being cognizant of himself and by a sort of prolongation of his cognizance of himself.

All that appears again, transposed and lessened, in Cartesian thought. But why is the soul easier to know than the body? Why does everything it knows reveal first its own nature to it? Not because its essence is the transparent object through which it sees all things, but because its glance stops at itself, ends in an idea which is something of itself, congeals in self-consciousness. My act of apprehension, as such, only grasps my thought, or a representation, an effigy depicted in it, with which, by reason of the divine truthfulness, some outward model corresponds. The idea thus becomes the sole term immediately attained by thought, the thing, portrait or representation, itself first known before making anything else known.[48] This reification of ideas, this confusion of the idea with an "instrumental sign" and an "object *quod*" is, as we have shown elsewhere, the original sin of modern philosophy.* It governs all the Cartesian doctrine of knowledge, the Cartesian first proof of the existence of God, the Cartesian theory of eternal truths; without it, Descartes as a philsopher is unintelligible.

* *Réflexions sur l'Intelligence*, chaps. II, III and IX.

Now it is curious to note here, yet again, a collusion with the angelic world. The divine ideas, in the light of which the Angel knows external objects, are creative or operative ideas, an artist's ideas: models in imitation of which a thing is made (*forma intelligibilis ad quam respiciens artifex operatur*). The object seen in such an idea is not a nature drawn from external objects and transported into the knowing spirit, it is a model issuing from the creating spirit, according to which the thing is placed in being. Confuse these ideas of the divine art with the concepts of human knowledge, and for both it will mean going from the idea to the object from thought to being, and you will have made of the object immediately grasped in the concept something different from what is:—a model, a picture of what is. You will thus have come back to the Cartesian ideas and the principle of all modern idealism.

With this theory of representational ideas the claims of Cartesian reason to independence of external objects reach their highest point: thought breaks with Being. It forms a sealed world which is no longer in contact with anything but itself; its ideas, now opaque effigies interposed between it and external objects, are still for Descartes a sort of lining of the real world. But as Hamelin says, the lining was to consume the cloth. Here again Kant finishes Descartes' work. If the intelligence when it thinks, reaches immediately only its own thought, or its representations, the thing hidden behind these representations remains for ever unknowable.

14. The retreat of the human mind on itself, independence of the reason with respect to the sensible origin of our ideas, to the object as the rule of our science, to

real natures as the immediate term of our intellection
—absolute intellectualism, mathematicism, idealism—
and, finally, irremediable breach between intelligence
and Being—that, then, is how Descartes revealed
Thought to itself.

The result of a usurpation of the angelic privileges,
that *denaturing* of human reason driven beyond the
limits of its species, that lust for pure spirituality, could
only go to the infinite: passing beyond the world of
created spirits it had to lead us to claim for our
intelligence the perfect autonomy and the perfect
immanence, the absolute independence, the *aseity* of
the uncreated intelligence.* Of that claim, Kant was
the scholastic formulator, but the origins lie much
deeper: and though the world's experience has
already been wretched enough and humiliating
enough to give it the lie, it remains the secret principle of the break-up of our culture and of the disease
of which the apostate West seems determined to die.

The old philosophy knew the nobility of the intelligence and the sublime nature of thought. It knew
that in its purity, and freed from every condition alien
to its formal notion, it is only fully realized in the
infinitely holy God. It knew that if the human
intelligence is the last of the intelligences, it yet par-
takes of the life and liberty which belong to the spirit;
that if it depends on the senses, it is to draw from them
wherewith to transcend the whole sensible universe;
that if it depends on the object to which it is proportioned, it is to gush out in spontaneous action and

---

* It is not without interest to note that, from a very different point
of view, Hamelin also observed that Cartesian innateness "is the
independence, the aseity, the sufficiency of thought." (Op. cit. p. 176.)

become all things; that if it depends on the being which makes it fruitful, it is to conquer Being itself and rest only in it. You pay dear for rejecting these truths.

That which is the measure has, as such, that which is measured under its complete rule, imposes its specification upon it, holds it bound and subject. Because it no longer understands the life which belongs to it as a created spirit, which interiorizes within itself what is its measure and finds its true liberty in that subjection, and because it wants an absolute and undetermined liberty for itself, it is natural that human thought, since Descartes, refuses to be measured objectively or to submit to intelligible necessities. Freedom with respect to the objective is the mother and nurse of all modern freedoms; it is the finest achievement of Progress, which makes us, as we are no longer measured by *anything*, subject to anything whatever! Intellectual liberty which Chesterton compared to that of the turnip (and that is a libel on the turnip), and which strictly only belongs to primal matter.

Thus the Cartesian reformation is not only at the source of the torrent of illusions and fables which self-styled "immediate clarities" have poured on us for two centuries and a half; it has a heavy weight of responsibility for the immense futility of the modern world and that strange condition in which we see humanity to-day, as powerful over matter, as informed and cunning to rule the physical universe, as it is weakened and lost in face of the intelligible realities of which the humility of a wisdom subject to Being once made it partaker. To fight against bodies it is equipped like a god; to fight against spirits it has lost all its weapons, and the pitiless laws of the metaphysical universe crush it in mockery.

§ III. CONTINUATION AND END

15. I apologize for having dwelt so much on the Treatise on the Angels in this attempt to discern the spirit of Descartes. It was very necessary to show that the word "angelism" is not a more or less picturesque approximation, but that it designates the special character of the Cartesian reformation in the metaphysical order, and that a number of the clearest and most precise analogies between Descartes and the angelic knowledge can be found.

The Angelic Doctor, when he elucidated, in one of the most splendid parts of the Summa—in that very part which the philosopher of the *cogito* heavily derided in front of young Burman, thinking himself witty, but only betraying, as he would have said, his own incompetence in the subject[49]—when he elucidated, as a metaphysician who knows what thought is, the properties of pure spirits, he not only introduced us to the best philosophy of the intellectual life, but prepared for us the means of penetrating the deepest meaning of the reformation of the human mind effected by Descartes, and of showing the true face of the masked reason which then moved on to the world's stage.[50]

Luther bore witness that it was the devil in person who convinced him of the inanity of the Mass. The "Genius" who taught Descartes was more wary. But what man in his sober senses could imagine that pure spirits are indifferent to philosophers, and only set themselves to control sorcerers? At the source of the error conceived by Descartes by his German stove it is very curious to note the simple application to human reason of the collection of properties and characteristics which are true of the physiology of separated forms.

We must not forget the importance of the stake. We must not forget that Descartes finally reversed the order of human cognition and made Metaphysics an introduction to Mechanics, Medicine, and Ethics, from which we shall henceforth gather the invigorating fruits of learning. In the higher order of Cognition, the Cartesian reformation gave the irretrievable stability of the things of the spirit to the moral attitude of turning towards perishable goods. See what the great name of Science has since become. It is to-day hardly applied to anything but the knowledge of matter, and science, *par excellence*, is regarded by most modern thinkers as belonging to a museum. In the modern world, reason turns its back on eternal things and is ordered to the creature. It rates the mathematics of phenomena above theology, science above wisdom. From the mountain of its excellence it has descried all the kingdoms of the material universe and the glory of them, and it goes down to possess them.

16. I do not claim that one can reduce to this *angelism*, or deduce from it, the whole of Descartes's doctrine. So complex a system involves a number of primary aspects and principles. We will not speak of the contributions of scholasticism (of a scholasticism, moreover, more or less pure). The taste for simple and easy strictness, for a venture strongly and reason-

ably conducted, a healthy aversion for pedantry and empty contention, a brave resolution to save the deposit of naturally Christian truths by force of good sense, by some quite simple and well worked out piece of boldness, closely relate Descartes to the best minds of his time. The naturalist and utilitarian tendency of his wisdom, the harsh and zealous love he vowed for his Physics, his radically mechanistic conceptions, his showy and reckless cosmology, which the Newtonians were to call the "romance of nature," all that belongs at once to the powerful physico-mathematical movement, which had been a passion with learned Europe for half a century, and to the gifts of his astonishing analytical genius which made him the initiator and prince, not of physical experiment, in which Pascal towers above him, but of all modern theoretical Physics. Descartes's angelism is, to my mind, only the deepest spiritual and metaphysical *intention* of his thought. It remains the fact that there would be no difficulty in showing how well the articles of his system derive from this secret principle. His dualism, in particular—which makes man, despite vain efforts to maintain the old notion of the substantial unity of the human compound, a complete spiritual substance (this as much from the point of view of specific nature as from that of subsistence) joined in an absolutely unintelligible manner to an extended substance which is also complete and exists and lives without the soul—is only the translation into the order of Being of a doctrine which, in the order of knowledge, attributes to the human soul the functions of the pure spirit. We can also note in what concerns Descartes's mechanicism that, for a human reason made angelic, before which all the secrets of the material world lie open, a Physics which is nothing but Geometry was the only possible physics.

17. But the quality of Cartesian angelism is again best shown in its remote consequences, in the fruits of an ideal logic decanted by time.

The very notion of the rational animal takes a turn to the divine after Descartes. The inhuman breach by which the modern age feels itself, as it were, mystically obliged to free itself from the past, is only explicable if we understand that at the dawn of this age an angel began to emerge from the chrysalis of humanity.

And so, while the novelties of the Renaissance and the Reformation were introduced in the name of an antiquarian zeal for the pure springs of former days—classical antiquity and the primitive Church—the sense of the worth and rights of what is modern, as modern, springs into life with the Cartesian revolution. We know well the part played by the Cartesians in the quarrel of ancient and modern, the Georges Sorel has well shown the Cartesian origins of the dogma of Progress.

Man is a political animal because he is a rational animal. If we go some distance in his chief operation, which is the operation of the intelligence, he does not naturally need to be taught, but should, as a perfect intellectual nature, proceed by the way of discovery alone, the deepest root, and the most spiritual, of sociability disappears. In spite of a strong personal attachment to discipline and authority in politics, Descartes is thus in a very high sense at the origin of the individualist conception of human nature. From afar, but most certainly, he paves the way for the man of

Jean-Jacques. Nor is his *rationalistic naturalism* without proclaiming in its fashion the naturalism of negative education. Is not Nature—leaning, it is true, on the philosopher's complete works—is not Nature enough for the building up of knowledge, and common sense enough for the approach to the most rare sciences? Now we have human nature quite naked, naked as a pure spirit, and reason *in the state of nature*, without the outward helps of human experience and the traditional *magisterium*, without the inward helps of the *habitus* and the virtues developed in the depth of the intellect, charged to scale the metaphysical heaven, until it sets itself to govern its own history and make happiness and goodness reign in the world.[51]

How, finally, should we not find in the transference of the angelic independence of external objects to our understanding the spiritual principle not only of idealism but also of rationalism properly so-called? The essence of rationalism consists in making the human reason and its ideological content the measure of what is: truly it is the extreme of madness, for the human reason has no content but what it has received from external objects. That inflation of reason is the sign and cause of a great weakness. Reason defenceless loses its hold on reality, and after a period of presumption it is reduced to abdication, falling then into the opposite evil, anti-intellectualism, voluntarism, pragmatism, etc. It must be a very superficial inquiry which would classify under a single heading, as M. Louis Rougier lately tried to do, such a malady of the mind and the great realism of the *philosophia perennis*—which smashes rationalism as roughly as anti-intellectualism and, because it respects the natural humility of the reason, allows it to go forward victoriously in the knowledge of Being.

18. As the Lutheran Reformation is the great German sin, I have said that the Cartesian Reformation is the great French sin in the history of modern thought. Truly Descartes gave a philosophic and rational *form*, and, by the same stroke, a spiritual consistence and indefinite vigour of expansion, to tendencies which were prevalent in Europe before him under very difficult aspects. This remains true, that France has made the success of the Cartesian philosophy, and thus allowed those tendencies to penetrate inside Catholic thought. It remains true that if the most subtle and most profound principle of the Cartesian philosophy, as I have tried to expose it in this study, came down from the land of pure spirits—a land, need we say? essentially cosmopolitan,—it has fallen on earth and germinated in our home climate. I am well aware that the triumph of Cartesianism in France marked the first crack in our house, recently rebuilt and beaten by all the winds of Europe. Yet much more than the ideology of the eighteenth century, all contaminated by influences first English, then German, Cartesianism is in the image, not of the French spirit—I would not advance so foolish an idea—but of certain typical deformities against which we have to be on our guard; in the image not so much of what is life and moderation in us, but especially of what is excess and weakness.

Let no one characterize it as the model of French thought: it still keeps much of its native strength, but its features are thinned and stretched even to grimace. Nor should we have the frivolity to see in it with M. Lanson the vivifying principle of our classical art.

On this point Brunetière was right: "The influence of
Cartesianism in the seventeenth century is one of the
inventions, one of the errors with which Victor Cousin
formerly infested the history of French literature."*
Moreover the direct influence of a philosophical
system on the arts is always very sporadic and superficial; it only truly makes impression on them indirectly
in consequence of the effect it has on the general
intellect,—and then with notable delay. We must seek
the Cartesian brand in literature in the last years of
the seventeenth century and at the beginning of the
eighteenth, at the time when La Motte was sorry that
Homer and Virgil had written in verse, and when that
poet—one of the finest geniuses France possessed,
according to Fontenelle, Mme. de Tencin, and the
Abbé Trublet—sang:

> La nature est mon seul guide;
> Représente-moi le vide
> A l'infini répandu;
> Dans ce qui s'offre à ma vue
> J'imagine l'étendue,
> Et no vois que l'étendu. . . .
> La substance de ce vide
> Entre ce corps supposé
> Se répand comme un fluide;
> Ce n'est qu'un plein déguisé.†

A little later Abbé Terrasson was to announce, "No
man who does not think in questions of literature as

* _Évolution des genres_, p. 46.
† Nature only is my guide; Show me emptiness infinitely diffused;
in what presents itself to my sight I imagine extension, and I see only
what has extension. . . . The substance of this emptiness spreads
through this assumed body a like fluid; it is only a fullness in disguise.

Descartes told us to think in questions of Physics is worthy of the present age."

All we can grant is that there are correspondences, because they have common causes, between the Cartesian philosophy and the parts of less resistance, or of less fullness, of an art whose substance and virtues depend on very different principles and have their origin in the twofold treasure, ancient and Christian. If Cartesianism attached itself to the fine working reason of the age of Louis XIV, it was to be its parasite. It was not Racine, nor La Fontaine, nor Boileau, it was their opponents, who sucked the milk of Descartes. It was Perrault, who wrote seriously, "Plato is condemned: he does not please the ladies," and stirred up the sex against Boileau. ("Don't be disturbed," said Racine to his friend, "you have attacked a very numerous body which is nothing but tongue; the storm will pass.") It was the *gentlemen* whom Racine recalled to respect for antiquity: "I advise these gentlemen no more to make up their minds so lightly about the works of the ancients. Such a man as Euripides deserved at least their examination, since they were anxious to condemn him. They should remember those wise words of Quintilian: '*Modeste tamen et circumspecto judicio de tantis viris pronuntiandum est*'." It was the "Hurons" and the "Topinambours" of the Academy, who were imperilling the classical deposit—"the whole thing is that they all club together against Homer and Virgil, and especially against good sense, as against an ancient, much more of an ancient than Homer and Virgil."* Whether it is authentic or not the saying attributed to Boileau is

---

* Letter from Boileau to Brossette (ed. Berryat Saint-Prix, III, p. 326.)

still very significant: "I have often heard him say
to M. Despréaux," wrote J.-B. Rousseau to Brossette
on the 14th July, 1715 "that Descartes' philosophy
had cut poetry's throat." How many other pallid
victims were already lying in the street!

.   .   .   .   .

19. The Cartesian angel has aged a good deal, he
has moulted many times, he is weary. But his undertaking has prospered prodigiously, it has become
world-wide and it holds us under a law which is not
gentle. He is an obstinate divider and he has not
only separated modern and ancient, but he has set
all things against each other—faith and reason, metaphysics and sciences, knowledge and love. The intelligence turned by him to the practical utilization of
matter overflows in action which is external, transitive,
and also material. And by that poor thing, the intelligence replaces the normal complement of its true life,
which is the immanent and spiritual activity of love;
for knowledge is only truly perfect when it flows out
in love. The world sighs for deliverance; it sighs
for wisdom, for the wisdom, I say, from which the
spirit of Descartes has led us astray, for the wisdom
which reconciles man with himself and, crowned with
a divine life, perfects knowledge in charity.

ROUSSEAU

or

NATURE'S SAINT

ROUSSEAU

or

NATURE'S SAINT

Dic ut lapides isti panes fiant. (*Matth.*, iv, 3.)
"If my husband is not a saint, who is?" (*Thérèse.*)

§ I. THE SAINT

1. THE Angels, who see all the happenings of this universe in the creative ideas, know the *philosophy of history;* philosophers cannot know it. For history itself is not a *science,* since it has to do only with individual and contingent facts; it is a memory and an experience for the use of the Prudent. And as to detecting the causes and supreme laws working through the stream of incident, to do that we should need to share the counsel of the supreme Fashioner, or be directly enlightened by Him. That is why it is properly a prophetic work to deliver to men the philosophy of their history. Herder and Quinet knew that when they mounted their tripod; and it is even surprising to discover how much an age of prophesying was the nineteenth century (which is at first sight the age of positive knowledge), just in so far as it was enlightened by Philosophers of History.

The Philosopher who is content to be not *more than human,* as Descartes says, hurling an arrow at the accursed theologians, will then deal with the philosophy of history only with a sense of the inadequacy of his resources to the matter under consideration. And if he rises above simple rational empiricism, which is confined to ascertaining proximate causes and is less philosophy than political science, he will not hope to reach certain inferences except so far as the events which he is judging receive their form from the history of ideas and thus share in its intelligibility. There indeed, in the charting of intellectual streams, absolutely solid mental judgements may become possible, by logical necessity and the objective meaning of the concepts.

Yet we must beware of a mistake. When we seek to discover in history the evolutionary line of a spiritual force, we must obviously consider this force as a *ratio seminalis* causing a development with various forms, conditioned at once by its own internal logic (*formal* causality) and by the human accidents on which it depends (*material* causality). What we have to do, then, is to ascertain the course of spiritual forces passing through men, with all kinds of unforeseen outbursts and fresh starts and great apparent breaks, rather than the direct relations between man and man.

Was not Rousseau, for instance, for years a Catholic, steeped in Catholic feeling? Did not Mme. de Warens pass on to him the dubious quality of a quietism which she in turn had debased? Are there not, besides, obvious oppositions between the optimism of Jean-Jacques and Lutheran pessimism? Yes; but that does not destroy the fundamental analogies which, despite the complete difference of manners and condition, make the spirit of Rousseau a revival of the old spirit of Luther. This spiritual filiation is far more worthy of consideration than the historical tie linking Rousseau to Calvinism by his early education.

Once the "evangelical" revolution was complete, and spiritual authority had passed to the princes along with the goods of the Church, the spirit of Luther had been quickly bridled in Germany by wholly external disciples and mere governmental utility; but deep in Protestant hearts it was still active. It takes the offensive again with Lessing, it carries all before it with Rousseau. Rousseau really did a work in the sphere of natural morality of the same type as Luther's work in the evangelical sphere. The Germans made no mistake about it, and the *Sturm und Drang* revived the disorders and delirium which had hailed the advent of the Reformation. But Luther's assault was on the high realms of grace. Rousseau attacked the sensitive and animal element in the human being.

It is manifestly absurd to show the Renaissance, the Protestant Reformation, the Cartesian Reformation, the Philosophy of Illumination, the Rousseauism, as a *unilinear* series ending in the apocalypse of the French Revolution. This systematization, used by rationalist historians hymning the stages of modern emancipation, arbitrarily conceals essential differences and deep oppositions. Yet to refuse to see the final convergence of these same movements would be an equal misconception of reality. We are faced by breaches at different points, and powers, intersecting and entwined, but tending in fact to the destruction of one same order and one same life. They are then one, at least in negation. It is even possible to find common characteristics and principles in these different spiritual currents, so long as we regard them as analogically, not univocally, common. In them there pass before us, in very different proportions and under forms often opposed

—naturalism, individualism, idealism, or subjectivism
—all the -*isms* which adorn the modern world.

2. Jean-Jacques Rousseau is no mere theorist of the
philosophy of feeling, like the English moralists of his
time, who are rather intellectuals and analysts dis-
coursing on feeling. It has often been noticed that he
himself—and how intensely!—is all feeling. He lives
in every fibre of his being, with a kind of heroism, the
primacy of feeling.

Does that mean that reason plays no part in him?
By no means. Reason in such a man plays a twofold
part. Sometimes it serves passion, and then it displays
a prodigious talent for sophistry. That is the moralizing,
stoical, plutarchian Jean-Jacques, pompous with virtue,
censor of the vices of his age, the Rousseau of the
Discours, of the letter to d'Alembert, and the *Contrat
Social*. Sometimes reason, like an ineffectual light,
watches the intoxications of evil desire and sees clearly
the harm of them. But it takes care not to interfere,
and watches always, and so really only increases the
attraction by giving it a certain flavour of intelligent
and *artistic* perversity since, as Aristotle says, it is
a mark of the artist to remain an artist when he *sins
deliberately*.

That is the Jean-Jacques of the "weak soul," the
"indolent" Jean-Jacques, the true Jean-Jacques, who
resists no allurement, who weakens and yields, who
surrenders to pleasure. He sees that he does ill, and
keeps his eyes raised to the image of the good; and he
delights at the same time in the good he loves but does
not, and the evil he does and hates not. That is the
Jean-Jacques who, protected by his good "mamma"
of les Charmettes from the perils of his age and leaving

the education of his purity to that pleasant teacher, at the very time when he is taking lessons from the generous lady, pours out to God his religious effusions and his love of virtue. Attacked by the moral deformities related in the *Confessions*, the husband of Thérèse in the sight of nature, the glowing confidant of Mme. d'Houdetot and her amours with Saint-Lambert, in all good faith he sets himself up as teacher of morals, vindicates the family and the home, and eloquently scourges adultery and the vices of the age. He starts the most violent revolutionary fables, and denounces with abhorrence the perils of revolution. He discharges into men's hearts in the *Nouvelle Héloïse* all the infections of voluptuousness, and makes Julie, when it is too late, calmly uphold the maxims of the most sensible and rational ethics. "Would you have one always consistent? One essay at least will bear good fruit!"* he himself said of the *Héloïse* and the stoical *Lettre sur les Spectacles* which are as opposed as white and black and were written at the same time.

Let us not reproach him. The "Father of the modern world" is an irresponsible. These contradictions are not in the least calculated, but are caused by his mental dissociation, and there is no deceit in them except the sorry cunning of a sick man to gratify his weakness and exploit it.

And we ourselves who judge him (*secundum hominem dico*), are we less full of contrasts, less ready to surrender? Dare we accept his cowardly challenge, which makes a covering for his pride out of the humility required of other people, and say: "I am better than that man"? If his public exhibition of himself disgusts us

* Second Preface (in Dialogue) to the *Nouvelle Héloïse*.

by its shamelessness, the sort of wretched tenderness which he arouses in us in spite of ourselves is not due solely to the admirable rhythm of his disclosure and its amazing lyrical flow. The reason is that he bares humanity in us and in himself, and thus awakens the natural sympathy which every being has for its fellow. The question is, whether he does not lead us to sympathize with just the lowest parts of our soul and what is most vitiated in the taste of our senses.

3. What is peculiar to Jean-Jacques, his special privilege, is his resignation to himself. He accepts himself and his worst contradictions as the believer accepts the Will of God. He acquiesces in being yes and no at the same time; and that he *can* do, just so far as he acquiesces in falling from the state of reason and letting the disconnected pieces of his soul vegetate as they are. Such is the "sincerity" of Jean-Jacques and his friends. It consists in never meddling with what you find in yourself at each moment of your life, for fear of perverting your being. So now all moral labour is tainted, from its source and by definition, with pharisaical hypocrisy: the last state of salvation without works! And it is wicked sophistry to confuse skill in *appearing* what one is not, with zeal to *be* more vigorously (that is, more spiritually), and to bring the great riot of what is less in us under the law of what is more.

We are not unaware that in our perverse hearts the virtue which is the work of reason alone, proud stoical virtue, usually has falsehood as its parasite. But we also know that the naïve hypocrisy nursed by Rousseauist sincerity is at least as deep and tenacious as the masked hypocrisy of the Pharisees; and above all we know that true virtue, the gentle virtue which in us is primarily the work of grace, as it grows, of itself drives all falsehood from the soul. Sincerity is the quality of what is pure and unalloyed. There is a "sincerity" of matter which would not be perfect, in the last analysis, except in isolation from all form, in pure dispersion, in pure potentiality. If it be true that man is man by what is the chief thing in him, that is, by the spirit, and that his specific sincerity, his sincerity as man, consists in purity of spiritual sight, by which he knows himself without falsehood (for sincerity, which is not simply purity, but purity of a knowledge uttered to oneself or another, can only strictly be understood by relation to the spirit)—then we must say that this sincerity of matter which plunges us in night and gives us over to all the dissociations of dream is the very opposite of true sincerity.

"You must be yourself"; in the last years of his life Jean-Jacques liked to repeat this formula.* On his lips it meant: you must *be* your feeling, as God *is* His being. Does God, Who is all act, need forming? You must regard as sin every attempt to form yourself, or allow yourself to be formed, to right yourself, to bring your discords to unity again. Every form imposed on the inner world of the human soul, whether it come from nature or grace, is a sacrilegious wrong to nature. The way in which Jean-Jacques is himself is the final resignation of personality. By dint of following the endless inclinations of material individuality, he has completely broken the unity of the

* Bernardin de Saint-Pierre: *la Vie et les Ouvrages de J. J. Rousseau,* ed. Souriau, Paris, 1907, pp. 98, 129, 183. Pierre-Maurice Masson: *la Religion de Rousseau,* vol. 2, p. 256.

spiritual self. The stuff no longer holds together. Man is no longer himself except at the price of dissolution.

The rationalist self had wanted to be self-sufficient. It refused to lose itself in the abyss of God, where it would have found itself, and now it can only seek itself in the abyss of sensitive nature, where it will nevermore find itself. Love, which was the panting of the spirit, and which presupposes as a condition of *self* surrender the *self* and its immanent life, has gone. Nothing but egoism remains and there is no *ego*, but only a stream of phantoms. Rousseau's man is Descartes's angel acting like a beast.

Rousseau brought into literature and real life that type of "innocent" in which the Dostoievsky of M. Gide (I speak only of *that* Dostoievsky, for the lesson of the other is perhaps less treacherous) found the highest grace. He foreshadows the great dissolution which we are asked to take for the wisdom of the East, and which, alien alike to Hindoo metaphysics and the old Chinese ethics, is only the mental collapse of a humanity in surrender.

4. If Rousseau's declamations bore us horribly, the interest of his life is always fresh. What is the most striking characteristic of his life, rich as it was in psychological lessons? To my mind, it is what one might call the MIMICRY OF SANCTITY—I do not say it was a studied comedy, I say, spontaneous mimicry, naïve, springing from the heart, *sincere duplicity*, whose first dupe was Jean-Jacques. Let us consider our hero from this point of view with due attention.

Concentrating in himself the heritage of all the loss of balance brought into the world since the Reformation, sick and ruined by neurosis, profoundly *asthenic*, a battlefield of exhausting hereditary contrasts, he unites with wonderful artistic gifts, with a quick intelligence, capable of remarkable instinctive good sense, with overstrung sensitiveness, with high desires and a flame of genius which shows in his wonderful eyes, an extraordinary impotence in the function by which man has rational mastery over reality. In the speculative order, every effort after logical and coherent construction is a torture to him; [52] "his various reasonings never harmonise except in the cadence of his lamentation,"* and, particularly, in the practical order, will, as a rational faculty, does not exist in him.

To realize a dictate of reason, to bring to being, to its own active being, a determination judged to be good, is impossible for him. He almost wholly lacks that act of practical reason which Thomist psychology calls the "imperium," [53] by which the intelligence, moved by the will, orders the executive faculties by a positive *fiat* to bring into the formidable world of existence what it has judged should be done. [54] As to the moral judgement itself, it is often good, even excellent, in him—at least, the "speculative" judgement which he forms when he consults his love of virtue. And what man does not love virtue, does not find it beautiful and good? That is an effect of the essential propensities of human nature, and that is why we are all so naturally led to require virtue in others. Now Jean-Jacques, who is not bothered by the world's maxims and the prejudices of false reason, the good Jean-Jacques of Nature, proclaims the theoretical love of virtue with more candour than anyone, nay, with a sort of cynicism.

* Charles Maurras: *Romantisme et Révolution, préface à l'édition définitive.*

But if it comes to forming a "practical" judgement, to making a resolution by reference to his own objects, to choosing for himself when confronted with reality what has to be done here and now, then reason capsizes and the attraction of the moment is so strong in him, so exclusive, that it makes him at once consider any attempt to reconcile the act to be performed on earth with the speculative heaven and its higher rules, to be absolutely impossible, and thus dispenses him from even the shadow of effort or struggle.[55]

It comes to this, that in Jean-Jacques there is no rectification of the will. Hence his vile actions and his moral weakness. That cowardice in face of reality is essentially the explanation of his abandonment of his five children and his crises of passion, his breaking of friendships, his impotent frenzies, the dubious "narcissism" of his opinions, and all the shames and wretchedness of his life.

And then? Then we are at the antipodes of the moral life and holiness! Agreed; but we see what happens. Incapable of imposing himself on reality by that supreme act of rational command without which there is no moral virtue, this perfect romantic stops at, and rests in the sphere of art, of the virtue of art, which is complete as soon as it makes a good *judgement* about what should be done. He judges then—and he judges well when there is no question of himself coming to a resolve *hic et nunc*—he judges, and does not act. And there, freed from all anxiety about performance, he merely dreams his life, builds it in the world of images and artistic judgements. And as he is a voluptuously sublime artist and has the love of virtue, and delights in the image of the good, the life he thus builds is an

JEAN-JACQUES ROUSSEAU
By HOUDON (*Château de Châalis*)

astonishing one of sweetness and kindness, of candour, simplicity, and easy sanctity without nails or cross. Is it, then, surprising that he is eternally maudlin about himself, and that Saint-Preux and Julie—that is, Jean-Jacques all the time—shed tears of pious and sincere enthusiasm over virtue just when they are surrendering to the least virtuous propensities? It is rather double personality than hypocrisy; but it is much more pernicious and more unhealthy.

5. Well, then, it only needs a favourable occasion, or an advance of the neurosis, for this imaginary world in which Rousseau spends most of his life to slip into existence in its turn, but, if I may say so, by guile; by way not of the moral will, but on the contrary of a more complete abandonment to the automatism of images, a final psychological cleavage.[56] Then, following the line of least inward resistance and the inclinations of the artistic will, Jean-Jacques will now let his dreams arrange his own life like a play, that life which he has given up all idea of shaping by the difficult effort of the moral will. First by strokes here and there, then at last systematically and continuously, he makes of his very being a deception, a simulation of perfection, a semblance of sanctity. "Nature has made of him nothing but a good *worker*, sensitive, it is true, even to ecstasy," he says of himself.* We must understand that the mental dominants of art, invading with the help of madness the whole field of the spirit, will at last take the place of all human development in him.

See him at the moment when, after his first Discourse, he sets up as recluse and copyist of music at ten sous a

* Second *Dialogue.*

page. He has made his timidity and his deep natural unsociability the very means of that radiation amongst men for which he had hitherto longed in vain, and he has found a sort of interior balance. He reforms, that is, he begins to dream no longer in imagination alone, but in action, to set his images free not only in his books, but in his life. "From then I became virtuous, or at least enraptured with virtue." "Everything helped to detach my affections from this world . . . I left the world and its pomps . . . A great revolution had just taken place in me, a different moral world was revealed to my eyes . . . I can date my complete renunciation of the world from that time."*

A reformation, certainly, but an artistic, not moral, reformation; the heart is still tainted and putrescent, thoroughly rotten with sensual self-love and self-complacency. He decides " to set all the powers of his soul to smash the fetters of opinion, and do bravely everything that seemed good to him, without troubling himself at all about men's judgement,"† but he declares immediately that this is "perhaps the greatest resolution, or at least the most useful to virtue, that ever mortal conceived," showing thus, as by the skilful publicity given to his undertaking, that he reforms for the public and not for himself. [57]   He affects a plebeian manner and plays the Christian cynic, but he is more than ever occupied with the effect which he produces on the world of nobility and wealth, which visits him constantly in his room and will soon applaud the *Devin du Village*. At last he is a model for humanity,

* *Confessions,* Book 8. cf. third *Rêverie,* and second letter to M. de Malesherbes.
† *Confessions,* Book 8.

a professor of virtue, a reformer of morals; and it is just at this very time that the future author of *Émile* abandons his third child.

See him after that in his last years, after the exile, after his great bitternesses and tribulations. He has fled from Hume and England, suffering from a real fit of madness, as he himself confessed to Corancez.[58] For three years he has wandered from town to town chased by the demons of honours and persecution. He is back in Paris, he is about to write the *Dialogues* and the *Rêveries*. He feels himself wrapped in a "work of darkness" whose "frightful gloom" he cannot in any way pierce and to which "all the present generation" conspires; he is surrounded by "triple walls of darkness," shut up in "the immense building of shadows which they have raised round him."* He knows that the whole world is in league against his person, that the conspiracy of philosophers has sworn his ruin, that he is forced to live "shut away from the society of men."† "The league is universal, without exception for ever; and I know I shall end my days in this ghastly proscription without ever fathoming the mystery of it."‡ Well, he pardons, he no longer answers his detractors, he behaves generously towards David Hume,[59] he does nothing beyond weeping over his misfortunes, over the "good works he has not been allowed to do,"§ over his unparalleled goodness of heart. Bernardin de Saint-Pierre is amazed at the simplicity and peace of his modest dwelling in the rue

* Third Dialogue. cf. 1st and 2nd Dialogue. *Confessions*, beginning of book 12.
† *Rêveries*, 2de Promenade.
‡ Ibid., 8e Promenade.
§ Ibid., 2de Promenade.

Plâtrirèe. Unselfish, temperate, gentle, indulgent, resigned, poor and loving poverty, he lives secluded, he has renounced the company of the great as well as the Armenian costume, he botanizes, he has entirely left the world. Doubtless he has not abandoned himself, and yet there truly is over him, at this moment, the shadow of greatness and true goodness. What has actually happened?

Actually, he has slipped finally into dream. Under the pressure of sorrow and tortures only too real, and a certain calming of desire brought by age, mental sickness has finished its work. Rousseau has broken, not every moral bond with the world, but every psychological bond with reality. Henceforward he can become indifferent, at least so he believes, to outer things, which are now nothing to him; no longer under restraint to reality—decompressed, if I may use the word—his imaginary self, his self of goodness, the self of his imagination and feeling, the self of his artist's dream unfolds in free relaxation. "If my husband is not a saint, who is?" Thérèse will cry after his death.* Jean-Jacques enters sanctity under full sail, his own sanctity, just when he is going mad, when he is entering the harbour of Dementia. He is indeed the saint of the age—do not all the pilgrimages to his grave bear witness to it?[60] The queen herself makes that pilgrimage. The sensitive souls come first, then the "good republicans" will come in their turn to the poplared isle of Ermenonville to shed tears on the "holy martyr's" grave, the grave of the "man of nature and truth," of "the man who never walked but in the paths of virtue," and venerate his relics, his snuff box, his shoes,

* Account of Pâris, the architect.

his cap. "The cap is the sign of liberty," cried Chérin to Montmorency in 1791, showing the crowd Jean-Jacques' cap, "and this one covered the head of the most illustrious of its defenders."*

It is in this sick genius, this empty sham, that the eighteenth century possesses its authentic model of virtue, whilst true sanctity begs on the roads in the person of another vagabond—a real poor man, this time.

Is there a more striking case of pathological counterfeit? A living and palpable phantom of goodness and wisdom, and inside it an understanding adrift, a will in ruins and incapable of the smallest rational recovery —and artistic gifts more beautiful than ever; pure

---

* *Masson*, vol. 3, p. 89. The reader should see the account of the pilgrimage which the Abbé Brizard (who ranked Jean-Jacques above Socrates) made to Ermenonville in July, 1783, with Baron de Clootz du Val de Grace (the future Anacharsis). After invoking heaven, the two pilgrims, when they got to Ermenonville, first go and sentimentalize over the holy relics. They fix little labels to them: "Jean-Jacques Rousseau's snuff box. . . . My fingers touched this box; my heart was thrilled, and my soul was the purer for it. Signed: Baron de Clootz du Val de Grace, defender of J.-J. Rousseau in my book *De la certitude des preuves du mahométisme*." "Shoes which Jean-Jacques Rousseau always wore. . . . G. Brizard wished to honour his name by hallowing it on the simple shoes of the man who never walked but in the paths of virtue." On the second day, they wander on the shores of the Lake, not without addressing "an ardent prayer to Saint Julie and Saint Héloïse." "It was from there that some virtuous Englishmen who had been refused a crossing threw themselves into the waves in order to touch the sacred land." The next day was employed in looking at the venerated grave from afar and singing hymns in honour of the "friend of morals." Finally, on the fourth day, judging themselves adequately prepared, they go over to the island, kiss the cold stone of the monument several times, and then as a sacrifice "to the shade of Jean-Jacques Rousseau," solemnly burn "the frightful libel" in which Diderot calumniates the saint. . . . "No," adds Brizard, "I shall not have made this pilgrimage to no purpose; it was not idle curiosity which led me to visit these regions; it was with the object of getting better acquainted with virtue." Everything here "so recalls to virtue!" For himself he feels "more confirmed in the ways of virtue" when he leaves Jean-Jacques' grave. (Abbé Brizard: *Pèlerinage d'Ermenonville. Aux mânes de Jean-Jacques Rousseau*. Masson, vol. 3, pp. 82 ff.)

surrender to the flow of dream waters, a soul fully, totally, supremely, swept by self-love.

6. He is holy: his holiness consists *in loving himself without comparison.** By one of those feats of psychological acrobatics of which only disease is capable, never having conceived his moral life as anything but a performance, he ceases to think of the opinion of others on the day when there is only himself to fill the auditorium. He ceases to order everything to his self on the day when his self has swallowed everything up; and thus egocentrism at its culminating point becomes capable of aping the unselfishness of charity. The self of Jean-Jacques has become *in itself* so interesting, so highly consoling, that it deserves to be contemplated and loved for itself alone, in all its parts and all its works noble or base, simply because it is; so immense that no obstacle can bruise it in future, so divine that it has no longer any contrary, so that Jean-Jacques loves himself too absolutely to have any self-esteem left,[61] that is, to envy or ask anything of others. "No more susceptible of modesty than of vanity, he is *content to feel what he is.*"† "I love myself too much to be able to hate anybody. That would contract, compress, my existence, and I want rather to extend it over the whole universe."‡ Watch him manufacturing his halo. "I doubt," he writes, "whether mortal ever said better and more sincerely to God: Thy Will be done."§ He is convinced that he is unique of his kind (like pure spirits), that he is the good man *par excellence*, the best of men; not that he is *virtuous*—he has re-

---

* Second Dialogue.
† Second Dialogue.
‡ *Rêveries*, IX, 370 (ed. Hachette).
§ Second Dialogue.

nounced that name since he yielded completely to his dream-self and by that became holy—but because he is *good*,* because he embodies in himself the Goodness of Nature (a distinction which will escape the pilgrims of Ermenonville and the devotees of the *holy martyr*). Let us read again the extraordinary prologue to the *Confessions*. "I am proposing an undertaking the like of which has never been, and of its performance there will be no imitators"; so much for modesty.

"I want to show my fellows a man in all truth of nature"; so much for Nature.

"And that man will be myself."

"Myself alone. I feel my heart and I know men. I am made like none of those whom I have seen; I dare to think that I am made like none that are. If I am not of more account, at least I am different. Whether Nature did well or ill to break the mould in which she cast me, can only be judged when I have been read."

So much for the "angelist" conception of the individual. And now for sanctity:

"Let the trumpet of the last judgement sound when it will, I shall come to appear before the sovereign judge with this book in my hand. I shall say boldly: This is what I have done, what I thought, what I was. I have told with equal candour good and ill . . . have shown myself just as I was: contemptible and vile, when I was so; good and generous and sublime, when I was so; I have revealed my heart as it was in Your eyes, eternal Being. Gather round me the countless

---

* Cf. *Rêveries*, 4*e* Promenade: "Happy if by my improvement of myself I learn to leave life, *not better, for that is not possible,* but more virtuous than I came into it."

multitude of my fellow creatures; let them hear my
confessions, let them lament my infamies, let them
blush for my meannesses. Let each of them in his
turn disclose his heart at the foot of Your throne with
the same sincerity, and then let but one of them say,
if he dare, *I was better than that man.*"

We may wonder at the way he confesses, and realize
what the Christian idea of confession has become in his
hands. He accuses himself, but only to give himself
absolution, the crown and the palm; if I may use the
phrase, he has turned Christian humility inside out,
like a glove. He finds himself quite at home with
the eternal Being. The fact is, that this eternal Being
is already really hardly more than a name for Conscience—hardly more than the immanent God of the
romantic philosophy. . . .

There are other passages. "I should go distrust-
fully," he wrote in 1763, alluding to a plan of suicide,
"if I knew a better man than myself. . . ."* And
again, after speaking of his failings: "With all that,
I am convinced that of all the men I have known
in my life none was better than I."†

What is to be said? He is right to proclaim himself
good, and we must believe him. He is in truth the
man of *natural goodness.* Is he not always innocent,

---

* Letter to Duclos, 1st August, 1763.
 † First letter to M. de Malesherbes. cf. again *Confessions*, Book 1:
"I think that never did individual of our species have naturally less
vanity than I." It was not safe to deny the goodness of Jean-Jacques.
"What? A man who spent forty years of his life loved by everyone
and without a single enemy is a monster? . . . The author of the
Héloïse is a scoundrel? . . . If there is any miserable fellow who can
believe that, it is he, Madame, who is a monster, it is he, who should
be stifled." (Letter to Mme. de Créqui, between 1772 and 1778. *Revue
de Paris*, 15 September, 1923: Unpublished letters of J.-J. R., collected
by Théophile Dufour.)

whatever he may have done, since he has never *willed* evil any more than he willed good? No one has realized to the same degree and so purely the kind of goodness of which human nature is capable when it overflows in pure spontaneous emotion, in a miraculous isolation from the order of reason and the order of grace. He shows us just what this *goodness* can and cannot do. From this point of view he is a unique and valuable specimen. Only we will add with the gardener's wife at Montmorency, "What a pity that so good a man wrote gospels!"*

At last he attributes to himself the privilege of being the still unblemished Man of Nature, without trace or stain of the original corruption due to civilization (this is what M. Seillière† calls his *immaculate conception*). And he becomes as God Himself: "All is over for me on earth. No one can now do me good or harm there. . . . And there am I, calm at the bottom of the abyss, a poor luckless mortal, but *impassible even as God*."[62]

Poor Jean-Jacques, detached from everything, truly, except from his exorbitant Individuality. We cannot help but pity him greatly, as we do Nietzsche, both of them victims, because they lived them to the very end, of principles of madness which they took from their age. (And they returned them to their age with interest.) But we must distrust this compassion. It

---

* Brizard: *Pèlerinage d'Ermenonville*, Masson, III, 86.

† Seillière: Jean-Jacques Rousseau, Paris, Garnier, 1921, p. 423. In our opinion M. Seillière's use of the word mysticism needs strong criticism; but anyone with an interest in Rousseau should be grateful to him for his studies (cf. "Le péril mystique dans l'inspiration des démocraties contemporaines," "Les étapes du mysticisme passionel," "Les origines romanésques de la morale et de la politique romantiques," "Mme. Guyon et Fénelon précurseurs de Rousseau"), and recognize their extreme importance.

must not mask from us the monstrous aberration of this
"self of sordid quality," "set up as just judge of the
universe," nor the catastrophes for which responsibility
lies on that "indignant and querulous sensitiveness
erected as a kind of law" and "the last court of
appeal"* against the order of the world.

Each one of us perceives dimly that the whole order
of the physical world is of less account than one spirit,
and that is why the wretched man is able to take us in.
The human heart yields. It thinks it hears the lamentation of a spirit, nay, some echo of the unutterable
lamentation which is the cry of the Spirit of holiness
in us, at which the joints of creation groan. It hears
only a vicious riot of flesh and blood.

7. Mimicry of sanctity, changing of the heroic life
into a religious enjoyment of self, ambition to reach
God and the divine life by sensation and the affective
imagination: is not Jean-Jacques the finest specimen of
the naturalist mysticism of feeling?

> "Let us hymn, exalt, the presence
> Of the new god of sensation"

cried Baumier in his *Tombeau et apothéose de Rousseau.*†

The idea which M. Seillière has formed of mysticism,
"an emotional and irrational enthusiasm confident of
union with a God," exactly fits Jean-Jacques Rousseau.
Moreover it only holds good for him and such as he.
Doubtless words are patient of everything. Yet there
is no more dangerous ambiguity than to group purely
and simply under the name of mysticism, without

* Charles Maurras: "Romantisme et Révolution," préface de l'édition definitive.

† Baumier: *Tableau des mœurs de ce siècle, en forme d'épîtres,* Londres
et Paris, 1788. (Masson, III, 76.)

indicating any *essential* difference, the love of a St. John of the Cross and that of an Amadis, the raptures of a Ste. Catherine and the transports of Jean-Jacques, Byron, Fourier, and Quinet; or even to give æsthetic or lyrical emotion as some sort of outline of the spiritual experience of the saints.* That is to change the meaning of language, to alter the currency of reason.

A great spiritual writer says, speaking of souls who have come to a very high state of abandonment and act by a different standard from human virtue under the impulse of the Spirit of Whom none knows whence He comes or whither He goes: "I hear all the virtues complaining that I am deserting them. The more pleasant these virtues appear to me, the more they draw me, the farther does the obscure impression which urges me seem to drive me from them. *I love virtue, but I yield to the attractions.*"† Put instead of a drawing from the Spirit of God the allurement of sensation and the emotional Dream, and there is Jean-Jacques and his detestable "similes." We may say that there is nothing of the true mystic in Rousseau, but that he is very mystical in the most depraved sense of that word. As M. Seillière very accurately says, he laicized quietism, and the extraordinary Dialogues written at the end of his life are only a lay transposition of the errors of Molinos and Madame Guyon. In them he develops on his own account a singular doctrine of absolute non-resistance to the impulses of sensation, a

---

* Lest we should understand in a dangerous sense authors who know far too much to fall into such a mistake, M. Brizard, for example, we must remember that there is an infinite distance between a *term of comparison* involving an *analogy* under some accidental aspect, but in a fundamentally and essentially different order, and an *outline*, however remote, imperfect and inaccurate it may be.

† R. P. de Caussade: *l' Abandon à la Providence divine.* Vol.   p. 115.

doctrine of complete passivity as the condition of full expansion of the primitive goodness, which is simply a natural quietism.

He then confesses that "Jean-Jacques is not virtuous"[64]—and this confession is itself a release for him, opening sanctity to him, as the confession that concupiscence is unconquerable had done for Luther. (It is true that it is the society of men which is to blame for the faults committed by so good a heart, by putting him in occasions of passion.) He confesses that Jean-Jacques, "the indolent Jean-Jacques" is "the slave of his senses" (adding moreover that "the sensual man is the natural man, the thinking man is the man of opinion: it is the latter who is dangerous, the other can never be so, even if he falls into excesses"). But if he thus ceases to put on virtue, if he gives up his former pretensions to a Stoic morality, it is because he is beyond virtue, he is *good*, he is "the primitive man." More than ever, then, he tends to the good, and his whole secret lies in opposing to the momentary inclinations which mislead us (and against which, moreover, there will be no active struggle) the most intimate and hidden tendency which is that of Nature herself,[65] which he imagines he sees directly, to which he refers as the inward Master, and by which he thinks he is divinely led. Too often he may have been "guilty," he has never been "wicked" (thus could Luther "sin", yet not cease to "trust"). He is united to Nature by goodness, as Mme. Guyon was united to God by grace; natural goodness is Rousseau's state of grace. He follows the gentle motions of Nature and the *inward feeling*, as Mme. Guyon believed she followed the divine instinct. He is confident of possessing the deifying gift of sensibility, as she of having charity. He escapes reality by the imagination, as she thought to get detachment from created things. He takes to dreaming, as she took to prayer. He is visited by his "inhabitants,"* as she believed she was visited by lights from above.

8. It was by spreading the contagion of that perverted religiosity over so many souls, that he gave the modern world one of its characteristic aspects. We all know what romanticism got from him.† *Irrequietum cor nostrum.* Rousseau plunged the heart into *endless* uneasiness, because he *hallows the denial of grace.* With the philosophers he rejected the gift of Him Who first loved us, but yet he makes an outlet for religious feeling. He turns our hunger for God towards the sacred mysteries of sensation, towards the infinite of matter. But he thus goes much farther than the romantic episode. Present-day thought, where it is diseased, still hangs on him. As the search for mystical enjoyment in things which are not God is an endless search, it can stop nowhere.

Only God's action is so determining as to join Being and Good everywhere, even in the filthiness of man's heart—absolutely all the Being and Good there is, yet

---

* On the "inhabitants" of Jean-Jacques, *see* Note 55.
† The word romanticism may give rise to many confusions. I am aware that there have been all kinds of things, even very good things, in the complex movement classed under this name. But nothing is so idle as to argue about words and recast their definition to suit your subject; and in spite of everything usage has adequately settled the meaning of this one. In so far as it signifies a religious eviction of reason and its works, the sacred unbridling of sensation, the holy parade of self, and the adoration of primitive natural instinct, pantheism as theology, and emotional stimulus as the rule of life, it must be confessed that Rousseau, by his mystical naturalism, is at the direct source of such a spiritual evil.

without the slightest touch of evil. In us there is at once complicity. There are regions of Being, which are good and desirable in so far as they are Being, and profit us to know, whose enjoyment is yet forbidden us by reason of the evil that frets them. It is no mere semblance that the saints renounce. They know what willingly they lose, and it must indeed be real if the hundredfold promised them be also real. All will be given back at the last end; there is no joy or love whose satisfying perfection is not offered to the heart in the beauty of God. Meanwhile we must hate our own souls and embrace the sweet cross. The desire enkindled by Rousseau casts the intelligence into an infinite world of perceptions, tastes, spiritual experiences, refinements, and ecstasies—sad as death, when all is said, but real for the moment—which are disclosed to us only in sin. There is spirituality of sin more treacherous than the vulgar attraction for pleasure of the senses. What holds the descendants of Jean-Jacques is the *spiritual savour* of the fruit of the knowledge of evil. To-day a deep attraction carries them towards the depths which they think more fertile than the heights, not understanding that only virginity is fruitful in the things of the spirit. And it is true that in these depths, in the "underground world" where the great discordant forces of unreason and instinct clash, there is still Being, reality, and life. It is true that this life is severely "bullied" by the order of reason; and it ought to be. For so long as man is governed only by the law of Nature and Reason, rebellion dwells in him with the law, and a part of his being must suffer violence. An unprofitable and fallen race, the truths of reason on which our existence hangs are burdensome to our existence, tormenting truths which should free us, but which crush us. How endure them, if a higher truth and a free gift did not divinize our life? "The best fate is not to be born, and to die is better than to live," said the highest pagan wisdom in the very act of affirming immortality. "When life knows not the ills which belong to it, then is it most free from sorrow. To be born, and thus to share in the nature of what is most excellent, is not the best thing for man; what is best for all men and women is not to be born, and after that, the chief of other possible goods, but the second of goods, is, having been born, to die as soon as may be. . . . Because existence in death is better than existence in life."*

The purely human order, the order of pure reason, is a harsh order, true and just, salutary and necessary, preserving Being, but deadly. Everywhere—under penalty of an infinitely harsher disorder—it involves limitation, constraint, the yoke, sacrifice to the good of the species or the common good. The executioner is a necessity for this order.

The order of charity does not destroy it, it confirms it; but it perfects it supernaturally, and without detriment to justice, imbues it with kindness. Then all is transfigured and renewed, every limitation turned to fullness, every sacrifice into love. If the fire of concupiscence is still there, necessitating constant vigilance, yet is man no longer rent. He is surrendered to the Spirit of God, and the great purifications and great nights into which this Spirit causes him to enter contain a divine fire and the liberating power of redeeming

* Aristotle: fragment of the Eudemian dialogue in Plutarch: *Consolat.* *ad Apollonium.*

love, even to the "underground world" of the soul
and its dark limbos, to the inward hell whose depths
only saints, at certain moments, have seen. Man has
received the peace passing all feeling, and he can hope.

Alas! The *invitatorium* that Luther chanted had
bidden to the marriage of the Lamb the creature without a wedding garment. At the Vespers sung by
Jean-Jacques he is already in outer darkness, naked
and gnashing his teeth, lost in self-enjoyment.

9. The ancients agreed that certain men are gifted
with a faculty of natural prophecy, in this sense, that
they are disposed to receive and perceive in their soul
the influences of higher cosmic agents. Let us say that
such men are prophets of the spirit of the world,
prophets of below, who concentrate in their heart the
influences which work in the deeps of wounded humanity during a whole epoch. They then proclaim the
age which is to follow them, and at the same time discharge on the future with prodigious strength those
influences which have found their unity in them. In
this sense, Luther and Rousseau do seem to be prophets.

Have they intellectual conviction, spiritual illumination, the example of an heroic personality? No. They
both act on men by an awakening of emotional sym-
pathies, by an astonishing diffusion of their material
individuality. They spread around them the contagion
of their self, the waves of their feelings and their in-
stincts, they absorb people into their temperament.
Jean-Jacques, from this point of view, has a quality
of impregnation, the greater that he is himself more
dissociated. The whole of the nineteenth century has
suffered this pathological impregnation. A stupendous
perverter, Rousseau aims not at our heads, but a little

below our hearts. He quickens in our souls the very
scars of the sin of nature, he summons the powers of
anarchy and weakness which lie dormant in each of us,
all the monsters like himself. He profits by all the
inadequacies of reason, manifested in such terrible
aggravation in the modern world, to hand our distress
over to the action not of grace, but of our lower nature.
Above all, he has taught our eyes to take pleasure in
ourselves and to connive at what they thus see, to discover the charm of those secret bruises of the most
individual sensitiveness which less impure ages left
with trembling to the eyes of God. "All the veils of
the heart have been rent," said Mme. de Staël of the
Nouvelle Héloïse. "The ancients would never have made
novels of their souls in this way." It will be a grievous
business for modern literature and thought, thus
wounded by him, to find again the purity and uprightness once known by an intelligence turned towards Being.

There are secrets of the heart which are hidden from
the angels, and open only to the priestly knowledge of
Christ. A Freud to-day attempts to force them by
psychological tricks. Christ looked into the eyes of
the adulterous woman and saw all, even the innermost soul; He alone could do so without stain. Every
novelist reads shamelessly in those poor eyes, and
brings his reader to the show.

§ II. SOLITUDE AND THE CITY

10. "I have a deep affection for the 'lonely walker'
in him; I hate the theorist." This saying of C.-F.
Ramuz[66] explains the attraction of Jean-Jacques for
many noble souls, and the echo he will always find,
even when they hate him, in those who, exempt from

his psychopathy, are yet his brothers in lyricism, "sensitive workers" as he was. Why that sympathy? Because of the dreams, tears, transports, sentimental tinsel à la Diderot? Nonsense! I am speaking of true lyricists. Because of the wild genius of a true spirit of the woods? Because of the fresh unfolding of a song genuinely springing from the heart of the solitudes, the purity of rhythm, without artifice and attuned to the movements of the soul, which is the only part of himself where Rousseau is truly innocent? Even that is secondary. The true reason is, as Ramuz again said, that before being an anti-social theorist Rousseau was born *non-social*, and that he has told incomparably the condition of a soul so made.

Men naturally respect anchorites. They instinctively understand that the solitary life is of itself the most exempt from the diminution and the nearest to divine things. Does not the tragic flight of old Tolstoy on the eve of his death come primarily from that instinct? And so many goings forth, so many wanderings? *Quoties inter homines fui, minor homo redii.* In differing degrees, philosophers, poets, or contemplatives, those whose chief work is intellectual know too well that in man social life is not the heroic life of the spirit, but the realm of mediocrity, and most often of falsehood. It is the burden of the unnecessary and the sham, from which poets and artists, as least free from what is perceived by the senses, suffer most sensitively, but not perhaps most cruelly. Yet all need to live by the social life in so far as the very life of the spirit must come out of a human life, a *rational* life in the strict sense of the word.

The solitary life is not human; it is above or beneath man. "There is for man a double manner of living solitary. Either he so lives because he cannot endure human society, by reason of the brutality of his temperament, *propter animi saevitiam*, and that belongs to beasts. Or else it is because he cleaves wholly to divine things, and that is of the superhuman order. He who has no dealings with others, said Aristotle, is either a beast or a god."* Extremes meet! Beast and god, the restless being who is but a fragment of the world, and the perfect being who makes up a universe in himself live an analogous life, whilst man is between the two, at once individual and person. As for Rousseau, paranoiac and genius, poet and madman, he leads at the same time and confuses voluptuously the life according to bestiality and the life according to intelligence. In this man, forced into solitary life by his physical blemishes, unfitted by his morbid shyness for the social régime, the unadaptability which rebels and complains, apes , the unadaptability which dominates, that of the spirit, *set apart to govern*, as Anaxagoras said of the *nous*. He gives us in his very unsociability, his sickly isolation, a lyrical image, as dazzling as it is deceptive, of the secret needs of the spirit in us.

11. But let us not forget the theorist. Making his personal misfortune the rule of the species, he will consider the solitary life to be the life natural to the human being. "The breath of man is fatal to his fellow beings; that is no less true strictly than figuratively," he declares.† Consequently the essential inclinations of human nature, and indeed the primordial conditions of moral health, require this blessed state of solitude which he pictures, projecting his own

* St. Thomas: *Summa Theol.*, 2–2ae, 188, 8 ad 4.
† *Émile*, Book I.

phantoms, as the perpetual flight through the woods of animals, dreamy, endowed with compassion, mating by chance meetings, and then going on with their innocent wandering. Such is the divine life in his eyes.

Thus the slip is immediate. The *supra hominem* has at once discharged into the bestial, not without giving it something of the sweetness of paradise. The conflict between the social life and the life of the spirit has become a conflict between the social life and savagery—and at the same time a conflict between the social life and human nature. By one stroke it has become an essential opposition, a harsh antinomy, absolutely insoluble.

What, however, does Christian wisdom say? It knows well that life according to the intellect leads to solitude, and that the more highly spiritual it is, the more apart is its solitude. But it knows also that this life is a superhuman life—relatively, with respect to the ways of rational speculation; purely and simply, with respect to the ways of contemplation in charity. That is the supreme end to be reached, the ultimate perfection, the last degree of the soul's growth. And for man to arrive at it, his progress must be in human environment. How should he go to the superhuman without going through the human? "We must consider that the state of a solitary is that of a being who should be self-sufficient; in other words, one who lacks nothing; and that pertains to the definition of what is perfect. Solitude, therefore, only befits the contemplative who has already come to perfection, either by the divine bounty alone, like John the Baptist, or by the exercise of the virtues. And man should not be exercised in the virtues without the help of the society of his fellow beings—with respect to the intelligence, to be

taught; with respect to the heart, that harmful affections be repressed by the example and correction of
others. Whence it follows that social life is necessary
to the exercise of perfection, and that solitude befits
souls already perfect."* That is doubtless why, in
very early times people ran to the desert to drag out
hermits in order to make them their bishops. . . .
Finally St. Thomas concludes "the life of solitaries,
if it be adopted rightly, is higher than social life;
but if it be adopted without previous exercise of that
life, it is most perilous unless, as with the blessed An-
tony and Benedict, divine grace supply what in others
is acquired by exercise."

Thus solitude is the flower of the city. Thus social
life remains the life natural to man, required by his
deepest specific needs. Its conventions and meannesses, the difficulties and lessening of the intellectual
life which it occasions, all the "pleasantry" which so
struck Pascal, remain accidental defects, which only
betray the radical weakness of human nature—the
price, sometimes terrible to pay, of an essential advan-
tage. It is social life which leads to the life of the spirit:
but by that very ordination, just as the activity of
the reason is ordered to the simple act of contemplation, so the social life is ordered to the solitary life,[67]
to the imperfect solitude of the intellectual, to the
solitude, perfect, at least interior, of the saint.†

* St. Thomas: *Summa Theol.*, 2–2ae, 188, 8.
† The life of *reason* as such, a life specifically human and postulating
things perceptible by the senses, in itself requires the social life; but in
so far as the speculative virtues make the activity of the reason a participation in the *purely mental* or *spiritual* life, in that degree it rises above
the social life. That is why the philosopher and the artist, because they
have an activity which is essentially rational (practical in the one,
theoretical in the other), are essentially involved in social life, and yet,

E

Hence harmony instead of an irreducible antinomy. The conflict is not suppressed (for that you would need to suppress man) : it is surmounted. Theoretically it is overcome perfectly; actually it is more or less overcome, according to our own state. The suffering remains, the opposition vanishes. Where is that seen better than where the harmony of social and spiritual is most purely realized, in that state of life specially established for the human conquest of perfection?

In the religious state, the very defects of social life work together for the good of the spirit. How is that? By the virtue of obedience, of a limitless sacrifice. Mistakes of government in superiors, mediocrity in environment, everything that man is capable of, and that a calced Carmelite can make a discalced Carmelite suffer, what do these accidents do but hasten the mystical death of a heart vowed to immolation? They cast it further into the divine life. So true is it that man has made peace with himself only on the Cross of Jesus.

12. Not in this way did Jean-Jacques undertake to resolve (for he fears nothing) the opposition which he himself made absolute and insoluble.

It is a flagrant absurdity, and at the same time an act of cowardly deceit, to treat men as if they were perfect, and the perfection which has to be acquired, from which most of them will always be far removed,

---

by what is most pure and valuable in them, overpass it and are urged to get free of it. The solitary life thus remains imperfect and virtual in them; they tend towards it, they have a foretaste of it, they snatch what they can of it from the jealousy of nature, it is not their own land.

The contemplative alone, leading a life which is essentially above reason, can perfectly lead the solitary life (yet not without holding on to social and rational life, but as a *condition*, which is prerequisite to his contemplation, or demanded by holy obligations—*praedicatio ex superabundantia contemplationis*).

as a constituent of nature itself. Yet such is Rousseau's principle, his perpetual postulate. This method of his is an astonishing system of vacuum cleaning, quite typical of his debility, and consists in passing at a leap to the conditions of absolute perfection or of the pure act. The geometrician refines the idea of stick or disc to define the straight line or circle. But Rousseau refines the human being of all potentiality, so that he may contemplate the ideal world, alone worthy of his thought, which will allow him to condemn in holiness the injustice of the existing world. He begins by placing himself in the unrealizable so that he may breathe and utter himself as God utters Himself in creation. He dreams, and he tells his dream; and if reality in no way corresponds with it, he cannot help it; it is reality that is wrong. "Only what is not, is beautiful,"* he delighted to repeat, in a formula which is metaphysically hateful. In 1765 at Strasbourg, a M. Angar procured an introduction to him in order to say to him: "You see, sir, a man who brings up his son on the principles which he had the happiness to learn from your *Émile.*" "So much the worse, sir," he replied, "so much the worse for you and your son!"† No, no, he knows better than we—it was his distinct intention—that all his idealogy is only a romantic piece of mechanism, and idle dream.

Rousseau begins, then, by assuming men to be in the pure exercise of their human activity. Then solutions come of themselves. And sublime ideas flow. Are you at a loss for the best form of government? It is that

---

* "One of the phrases he most constantly repeated, in speech and writing is this : 'Nothing is beautiful but that which is not.' 'D'Escherny: *Éloge de J.-J. Rousseau*, at the top of *l'Égalité*, 1796, I, p. lxxvii. Masson, II, 260.

† Cf. E. Seillière: *Jean-Jacques Rousseau*. Paris, Garnier, 1921, p. 132.

designed for the perfect: *"regimen perfectorum, ergo regimen perfectum,"** holy Democracy. Do you want a sound method of education? It is the one which requires: 1, princely conditions of wealth and isolation; 2, a single tutor for a single pupil; 3, an ideal tutor and an essentially good pupil—the hypocritical negative Education in which Nature (conveniently faked at a pinch) does all the work; all is perfect in it.

As to the social state, it must be built of self-sufficing individuals—who have not, so far, succeeded in coming together without sinking. "The wicked man lives alone," Diderot might well hurl this treacherous bolt at him. Jean-Jacques will suffer as an innocent victim, but will hold fast to his axiom: man would be good if he were alone. But if our nature, corrupted by the discovery of civilized life, has to be mended by the help of some more sublime discovery, he, Jean-Jacques, has the secret of the perfect city, built in his head with the perfect, that will restore man in a new way to the privileges of the state of solitude in the very midst of social life.

13. And behold, there rises before us the rich ideological forest of the *Contrat Social*. We will here enumerate, and try to express in a short formula which will give an idea of their essential spirit, the chief myths which the modern world owes to that famous work.

I.—NATURE.—In his limpid and subtle Treatise on Law, St. Thomas explains that the term "natural law" can be taken in two quite different senses. A thing can be said to be "of natural law" either because nature inclines towards it (as that one should not harm others),

---

* The sophism consists in stating that the *perfect government* is by definition the *government of perfect subjects*. On the contrary, government as such is the more perfect as it succeeds in ordering more imperfect subjects to the common good.

or only because nature does not at once assert the contrary arrangement. "In this latter sense it might be said that to be naked is *de jure naturali* for man, because it is art, not nature, which provides him with clothes. It is in this sense that we should understand Isidore when he says that the state of common possession and of one and the same liberty for all is *of natural law ;* in fact, the distinction of property and submission to a master are not things provided by nature, but introduced by man's reason as useful to human life."*

In other words, the word nature can be taken in the metaphysical sense of *essence* involving a certain finality. Then what is natural is that which answers the requirements and propensities of the essence, that to which things are ordered, by reason of their specific type and finally, by the Author of Being. And it can be taken in the material sense of an actual primitive state. Then what is natural is that which actually existed before all developments due to the intelligence.

The weakening of the metaphysical spirit was bound gradually to obscure the first sense of the word nature. In the radically nominalist and empiricist theory of Hobbes, followed in that by Spinoza, the second sense alone remains and, badly stated, leads the philosopher to logical errors. According to Hobbes, the absolute isolation of individuals is "natural"; so is the battle of every man against his neighbour which he takes to be the primitive state of humanity. And with the rational mystic's peculiar pessimism, Spinoza declares: "The natural right of each stretches as far as his power. Whoever is deemed to live under the sway of nature alone has absolute right to covet whatever he

* *Summa Theol.*, 1–2ae, 94, 5 ad 3.

considers useful, whether he be led to this desire by
sound reason or by the violence of the passions. He has
the right to seize it in any way, whether by force, by
cunning, by entreaty, by whatever means he considers
easiest, and consequently to regard as an enemy anyone who would hinder the satisfaction of his desires."*
Nothing could be clearer.

What does Jean-Jacques do? Because he is of a
religious disposition, and because withal what good
sense he has is solidly traditionalist, he returns to the
notion of nature in the first sense of the word, to the
notion of a nature ordered to an end by the wisdom of
a good God. But because he is powerless to realize
that notion intellectually, and restore to it its metaphysical value and range, he insinuates it into the
picture of a certain primitive and, so to say, ante-
cultural state, which exactly corresponds to the second
sense of the word nature. He muddles up these two
different senses, he locks into a single equivocal pseudo-
concept the "nature" of the metaphysicians and the
"nature" of the empiricists. Hence comes the
Rousseauist myth of Nature, which needs only to be
clearly expressed for its absurdity to be seen: *Nature
is the primitive condition of things, at which they should stop,
or which they should restore, to comply with their essence.*
Or again: *Nature is the essential need, divinely placed in
things, of a certain primitive condition or ante-culture which
things are made to realize.*

From this myth of Nature will come logically the dogma of Natural Goodness. All that is necessary is the
discovery that nature in the sense of the metaphysician,
the immutable essence of things, and particularly the

* *Tractatus theologico-politicus*, cap. xvi.

human essence with its faculties and specific propensities, is good. The conclusion will follow that the primitive state and the primitive conditions of human life, the state before culture and before the institutions of reason (whether it be pictured as formerly realized in history, or be conceived only as an abstraction), was necessarily good, innocent, happy, and that a state of goodness, a fixed condition of innocence and happiness, is due to humanity. . . .

Rousseau's discovery of the dogma of natural goodness dates from the writing of his *Discours*, after the revelation of the Bois de Vincennes and the coat wet with tears. In the *Contrat Social* which he wrote later, but from his old Venetian note-books, this dogma is not formulated, it is even sometimes contradicted. Yet the myth of Nature, which has the seeds of it, is certainly there. We realize that, when we remark that it is the myth of Nature that engenders the myth of Liberty, absolutely essential to the *Contrat Social*.

II.—LIBERTY.—"Man is born free." (A savage in a wood.) In other words, *the state of liberty or sovereign independence is the primitive state, whose maintenance or restoration is required by man's essence and the divine order.*

Henceforward no kind of submission to a master or lording over a subject is allowable. The condition which, according to theologians, prevailed in the earthly paradise, in which all were of free estate (that is, where none worked in the service of another and for the private good of another, because in the state of innocence there was no servile work), becomes the state required by human nature. Nay more, according to St. Thomas, the state of innocence must have involved that kind of domination over free men which

consists in guiding them towards the *common* good,—
"because man is naturally social, and because social
life is impossible unless someone be pre-eminent to aim
at the common good—"*multi enim per se intendunt ad
multa unus vero ad unum*"—and because, on the other
hand, if a man is eminent in justice and knowledge he
naturally serves the utility of others,* that is to say,
he governs. But Jean-Jacques, on the contrary, would
have us say that that very kind of sway is precluded by
nature. Man is born free, Liberty is an absolute
requirement of Nature, all subjection of any kind to the
authority of any manner of man is contrary to Nature.

III.—EQUALITY.—An equal condition for all is likewise required by Nature. All of us are born equally
men, and so equally "free," equal as to specific *essence*
and consequently (and this is the tremendous confusion
of thought peculiar to egalitarianism) equal in regard
to the State, whose realization for each individual is
required by our essence and the divine order. There are,
doubtless, so-called "natural" inequalities between
individuals more or less hardy, more or less intelligent.
But they are against Nature's desires, and who knows
if they do not go back to some remote malformation?

*Nature requires that the strictest equality should be realized
amongst men, so that, in every political state which is not
directly against Nature and her Author, an absolute social
equality should exactly balance natural inequalities.*

This myth of Equality is supported by two oddly
clumsy sophisms:

1. The confusion of *equality* with *justice*—which
destroys justice. Justice† indeed implies a certain

* *Summa Theol.* I, 96, 4.
† We are speaking of distributive justice (*totius ad partes*), the only
kind with which we can be concerned here

equality, but a *geometrical* or *proportional* equality (which treats both sides in proportion to their deserts), and not *arithmetical* equality or that of *absolute size* (which treats both sides the same, whatever be their deserts); so that to confound justice with that second species of equality, with equality pure and simple, is just precisely to destroy justice.

2. The confusion—which would render the constitution of any social body impossible—of what concerns *recompense* to parts with what concerns the *constitution* of the whole. St. Thomas explained this vigorously against Origen, the metaphysical patriarch of egalitarianism, who claimed that God must have created all things equal (for before being created they were all equally nothing), and that the diversity of things and the arrangement of the world came from the sin of the creature. He says that in the order of *retribution* justice should be exercised, and it demands that equal things should be rendered to equals, because in that order you must necessarily presuppose deserts. But in the order of the *constitution* of things, or of their *first institution*, these requirements of justice have not to be exercised, because in that order merits are not necessarily to be presupposed, but only a work to bring into existence, a whole to be produced. "The artist places in different parts of the building stones which are by hypothesis all alike, and this without wronging justice: not that he assumes in them some pre-existent diversity, but because he is aiming at the perfection of the whole thing to be built, which could not be if the stones were not placed in the building differently and unequally. Likewise, it is without injustice, and yet without presupposing any diversity of merits, that God from the

beginning established in His wisdom different and unequal creatures, that there might be perfection in the
universe."*   And in the same way, assuming by
hypothesis that all men are equal in worth, it is no
injustice that in order to establish the body politic—
and otherwise that body could not be—they should
be set in different parts of it and consequently have
unequal rights, functions, and conditions.

IV.—THE POLITICAL PROBLEM.—The myth of Liberty and the myth of Equality led Rousseau to formu-
late the political problem in a way which is wholly
and absurdly Utopian. How make a society with
individuals all perfectly "free" and "equal"? How,
to use Rousseau's own expressions, harmonize *men*
(such as nature would have them) and *laws* (such as a
social body requires)? *How "find a form of association
by which each being united with all should yet obey only
himself, and still be as free as before"* ?

It simply amounts to establishing an organic whole
without its parts being subordinate to one another.
That is absurd; but Jean-Jacques is happy. The more
difficult the problem, the more merit he will have for
devising the solution. His prophetic mission consists
in condemning and anathematizing the existent unjust
city, and showing men the only conceivable type of just
city. Is it impossible that this just city should exist?
Let the unhappy beings who are condemned to existence
get out of the business as best they can; they can always
"throw themselves on the ground and lament that
they are men," as Jean-Jacques himself does when he
despairs of democracy and remembers Caligula.

V.—THE SOCIAL CONTRACT.—It is the social contract

* *Summa Theol.*, I, 65, 2 and 3.

which "gives the solution" of the "fundamental problem" which has just been stated. *The social contract is a pact concluded by the deliberate will of sovereignly free individuals whom the state of nature formerly held in isolation and who agree to pass into the social state.*

Although it derives from it by a long progress of degradation which goes from Althusius and Grotius to Rousseau, this myth of the Contract is quite different from the *consensus* which the ancients allowed to have been at the beginning of human societies, and which was the expression of a natural aspiration. The Rousseauist contract has its first cause in the deliberate will of man, not in nature, and it gives birth to a product of human art, not to a work proceeding from nature; it presupposes that "the individual alone is the work of nature."

Hence it follows that the first author of society is not God, the Author of the natural order, but the will of man, and that the birth of civil law is the destruction of natural law. The ancients taught that human law derives from natural law as making specific what was left indeterminate by the latter. Rousseau teaches that after the pact there are no more natural rights, and it will be granted henceforth that in the social state there could be no right but from the agreement of free wills. . . .

But the notion of the Rousseauist contract is not yet complete. It is, indeed, not an indefinite covenant; it has a fixed nature, it implies essentially certain terms without which it is nothing and from which Jean-Jacques will deduce his whole system. *These terms can really all be reduced to a single one ; that is the complete transfer of each associate, with all his rights to the whole community.*

Where, then, is liberty? And how is the "fundamental" problem solved? Ah! That is just the wonder. "As each gives himself to all, he gives himself to no one"; he is subject to all, but he is subject to no man, and that is the essential thing, there is no man above him. Nay more, as soon as the covenant begets the social body, each is in such wise absorbed in that common self which he has willed, that by obeying it he still obeys himself. Then the more we obey, not a man— God forbid!—but the general will, the more free we are. A happy solution! In the state of nature we only existed as persons, in no way as parts; in the state of society we no longer exist except as parts. Thus does pure individualism, precisely by misconceiving the reality which belongs to the social bonds added to individuals by natural need, end inevitably in pure bureaucracy as soon as it undertakes to construct a society.

VI.—THE GENERAL WILL.—This is the finest myth of Jean-Jacques, the most religiously manufactured. We might call it the myth of political pantheism. The *General Will* (which must not be confused with the sum of the individual wills) *is the Common Self's own will, born of the sacrifice each has made of himself and all his rights on the altar of the city.*

Truth to tell, here there is a question of a kind of immanent God mysteriously evoked by the operation of the pact, of whose decrees the majority of votes is only a sign, a sacred sign which is only valid under certain conditions—particularly, Rousseau teaches, under the condition that no partial society exist in the whole.

Immanent social God, common self which is more I than myself, in whom I lose myself and find myself again and whom I serve to be free—that is a curious specimen of fraudulent mysticism. Note how Jean-Jacques explains that the citizen subject to a law against which he voted remains free, and continues to obey only himself: men do not vote, he says, to give their opinion; they vote that, by the counting of votes, the general will may be ascertained, which each wills supremely, since it is what makes him a citizen and a freeman. "When then the opposite opinion to my own carries the day, that proves nothing but that I was wrong, and that what I thought to be the general will was not so. If my private opinion had carried the day, I should have done differently from what I willed; and then I should not have been free." What does he hold out to us here but a preposterous transposition of the case of the believer who, when he prays for what he thinks expedient yet asks and wills chiefly that God's Will may be done?* The vote is conceived by him as a species of ritual petition and evocation addressed to the General Will.

VII.—LAW.—The myth of the General Will is central and dominant in Rousseau's political theory, like the notion of the common good in Aristotle's. The common good, as the end sought, essentially implies the guidance of an intelligence, and the ancients defined law as an arrangement of the reason tending to the common good and promulgated by him who has the care of the community. The General Will, which animates and moves the social body, imposes itself on all by its mere existence; it is enough for it to be, and it is shown by Numbers. *Law will then be defined*

---

* In the *Nouvelle Héloïse* (part III, letter 18) he cried to God: "Make all my actions in conformity with my steady will, which is Yours." The analogy of the formulas is curious.

*as the expression of the General Will, and it will no longer
proceed from reason but from numbers.*

It was essential to law as the ancients understood it
that it should be just. Modern law has no need to be
just, and it demands obedience all the same. Law as
the ancients understood it was promulgated by some
ruler; modern law is in sole command. As Malebranche's God reserved to Himself alone the power of
acting, so that mythical sign enthroned in the heaven
of abstractions reserves authority. Below it on earth
men are, from the point of view of the relations between
authority and submission, mere dust, alike and absolutely shapeless.

VIII.—THE SOVEREIGN PEOPLE.—The law only
exists in so far as it expresses the General Will. But the
General Will is the will of the people. "The people
who are subject to the laws, should be author of the
laws," for so they obey only themselves, and we are at
the same time "free and subject to the laws, since
they are only records of our wills."

*Sovereignty, then, resides essentially and absolutely in the
people, in the shapeless mass of all individuals taken together,*
and since the state of society is not natural but artificial,
it has its origin not in God but in the free will of the
people itself.*   Every state which is not built on this
foundation is not a *State governed by laws,* a legitimate
State; it is a product of tyranny, a monster violating
the rights of human nature.

There we have the true myth of modern Democracy,
its spiritual source, absolutely opposite to Christian

---

* If Rousseau sometimes repeats classical formulas which make
God the source of sovereignty, he does so either illogically, or because
he defies the will of the people.

law which will have sovereignty derive from God as
its first origin and only go through the people to dwell
in the man or men charged with the care of the
common good.

Notice that the question here raised is quite distinct
from that of forms of government. Although in themselves of unequal merit, the three classical forms of
government have their place in the Christian system,
for in democratic régime sovereignty will reside in
those chosen by the multitude.* And in the same way
they all three have their place at least theoretically in
Rousseau's system—and are all three equally vitiated
in it. "I call any State that is governed by laws a
republic (that is, any State where the laws are the expression of the General Will and where therefore the
people is sovereign), "*under whatever form of administra-
tion it may be. . . .* Every lawful government is" consequently "republican. . . . To be lawful, the government must not be identified with the sovereign, but the
minister of the sovereign; then monarchy itself is republican." The prince does not perform acts of sovereignty
but of "magistracy"; he is not the author, but the
minister of the Law, not a scrap of authority resides in
him, and authority is all in the General Will; there
is no man responsible for looking after the common
good, the General Will is adequate for that. In the
Rousseauist system, that holds good for the aristocratic
or monarchical régime, as for the democratic.

* *May* it not happen, as an extreme case, that in a very small group
(say a Swiss canton) and in very special conditions, the multitude itself
would look after its common good? Historical fact there sets Christian
law an interesting problem. In any case, the absurdity lies in turning
such an extreme possibility into a legal necessity imposed on every
form of government.

Yet, in fact, with Rousseau himself and in the world which he fathered, there is inextricable confusion between Democracy as myth and universal doctrine of sovereignty, and democracy as a particular form of government. There may be discussion as to whether the democratic form of government is good or bad for a certain people in certain conditions; but it is beyond dispute that the myth of Democracy as the sole legitimate sovereign, the spiritual principle of modern egalitarianism, is a gross absurdity.

IX.—THE LAWGIVER.—The people always wills the good, but it is not always sufficiently informed, it is even often deceived, "and then only does it seem to will what is bad." The General Will needs enlightenment. The immanent God of the republic is a child God who wants helping, like the God of the pragmatists. *The lawgiver is the superman who guides the General Will.*

Neither magistrate (for the magistrate administers the law already made), nor sovereign (for the sovereign who proposes the law, is the people) he is, for formulating and propounding the law, outside and above every human order, in the void. "The lawgiver is a man in every respect extraordinary in the State. If he should be extraordinary by genius, he is not less so by his work. That work founds the republic; it does not enter into its constitution; it is a peculiar and higher function which has nothing in common with human rule."

This amazingly hackneyed myth is not without its dangers. Let us listen to Rousseau and understand that his utterances are a perfectly logical consequence of his principles and of the doctrine which will not allow that man is *by nature a political animal.* "He who dares to undertake to found a nation should feel that he is in *a position to change human nature, so to say;* to *transform* each individual, who by himself is a perfect and solitary *whole, into* a part of a greater whole, from which that individual should in some measure receive his life and being; *to change man's constitution* in order to make it stronger. . . . He must, in a word, deprive man of his own powers, to give him powers foreign to him, powers which he cannot exercise without the help of others. *The more dead and ruined these natural powers are,* the greater and more lasting are those acquired, *the more solid and perfect* [sic] *too is the foundation;* so that if each citizen is nothing and can do nothing except with all the others, and the power acquired by the whole be equal to or greater than the sum of the natural powers of all the individuals, you can say that the legislation is as perfect as it could possibly be."

Everything in this valuable passage should be remembered and pondered. But what then is this extraordinary and extra-cosmic lawgiver? We have not far to seek. It is Jean-Jacques himself—Jean-Jacques who, quite meaning to be the perfect Adam who completes his paternal work by education and political guidance, finds comfort for bringing children into the world for the Foundling Hospital in becoming Émile's tutor and the lawgiver of the Republic. But it is also the Deputy (*Constituant*), and in general every city-builder on the revolutionary plan, and it is most precisely Lenin.

Such, very briefly outlined, are some of the fables of the *Contrat Social.* Their "mysticism," which looks reasoned and rational, is just as mad as the mysticism of sentiment and passion which we find in *Émile* and

the *Nouvelle Héloïse*. It is noteworthy that the former
had its chief success in France, where we have tried
it to our cost; whilst the second met with extraordinary
success in Germany, and in another sphere did amazing
damage.

§ III. DEBASED CHRISTIANITY

14. Jean-Jacques owes little enough to Calvin and
Calvinistic theology, at least directly. He is more
indebted to Geneva and Genevan civic zeal[68] and
still more to the climate of Lake Leman, to that
singular mixture of primitive simplicity, sensuality and
quietism, impassioned sensibility and inertia, which
seems to characterize the moral disposition of that
region. (From this point of view Rousseau, although
originally of French stock, remains profoundly Ro-
mansch.) What he owes to Calvin is his pretensions to
virtue, his moralism, his affectation of strict ration-
ality, so cruelly contradicted by his true nature, and,
above all, his attitude of continual *protest*, his inborn
mania for reproving other people's morals. To him
he also owes *privation* of the means of grace and truth
which, had it not been for the Calvinist heresy, might
have kept his inherited disposition in better balance.

On the other hand, his conversion to Catholicism
in that sad Hostel for Catechumens at Turin—the
description of it is, one would hope, over-gloomy—is
certainly more sincere than he makes out in his *Confessions*. I say, more sincere; I do not say more real
and deep. Of the faith and Catholic life he never
grasped anything but the outward air, the visible
show, on which his greedy sensuality, nowise subdued
but on the contrary irritated by being unsatisfied during

his Calvinistic childhood, fed to the full in the questionable atmosphere of Mme. de Warens. He did not return to Calvinism until 1754, so that he stayed in the Catholic Church for twenty-six years. Without this transit through Catholicism, without the misuse of holy things and divine truths of which his Catholic culture made him capable, Rousseau would not have been complete, there would have been no Jean-Jacque. I willingly grant that. But I add that he passed through Catholicism as certain pathogenic ferments pass into an organism or a culture to increase their virulence.

Rousseau had a religious disposition. He always had great religious needs, and we may say that by nature there were much richer religious dispositions in him than in most of his contemporaries (but what are the finest religious dispositions without supernatural life?) It is by that strong religious quality that he has worked on the world. Although himself too busied with his single self, too fantastic and too lazy, ever to have wanted to assume the responsibilities of such a part, yet really he is essentially a religious Reformer.

That is why he could only take his full flight by passing through the Church, the better to purloin the words of life. It is the Gospel, it is Christianity, that he debases and uses.

He perceived great Christian truths which his age had forgotten, and his strength lay in recalling them; but he perverted them. That is his mark, and that of true Rousseauists: corrupters of hallowed truths. They know how to loose them from their vows—they, too, were "blessed robbers," as Luther said so boastfully. When he reacts against the philosophy of illumination; when he proclaims the existence of God, of the soul,

of Providence, against the philosophers' atheism; when
he invokes against the critical nihilism of their vain
reason the worth of Nature and her primordial tendencies; when he justifies virtue, candour, the family,
civic devotion; when he affirms the essential dignity
of the conscience and human personality (an affirmation which was to have so lasting an echo in Kant's
mind), then Rousseau is displaying Christian truths
to his contemporaries. But they are Christian truths
emptied of substance, of which nothing is left but
the glittering husk. They fall in fragments at the first
blow, for they no longer derive their existence from
the objectivity of reason and faith, they no longer
subsist except as expansions of the subjectivity of the
appetite. They are puffed out and drivelling truths,
declaring Nature absolutely good in every way, reason
incapable of reaching truth and capable only of cor-
rupting man, conscience infallible, the human person
of such worth and so divine that it can validly obey
nothing but itself.

Above all—and this is the most important point—
Jean-Jacques has perverted the Gospel by tearing it
from the supernatural order and transporting certain
fundamental aspects of Christianity into the sphere of
simple nature. One absolute essential of Christianity
is the supernatural quality of grace. Remove that
supernatural quality, and Christianity goes bad. What
do we find at the source of modern disorder? A *naturalization* of Christianity. It is clear that the Gospel,
rendered purely natural (and, therefore, absolutely
debased), becomes a revolutionary ferment of extraordinary virulence. For grace is a *new order* added to
the natural order and, because it is *supernatural*, per-

fecting without destroying it; if that order of grace be rejected in so far as it is *supernatural*, and its shadow retained and imposed on reality, then at once the natural order is upset by a self-styled new order which would take its place. Thus did Luther, who with his nominalist theology completely confused nature and grace, want to *exterminate reason* in order to save faith. And Kant likewise was to say: "I had to suppress knowledge to make room for belief."

It is an axiom of the peripatetics that every higher *form* contains in it, in the state of unity, the perfections distributed severally in lower forms. Apply that axiom to the Christian *form*, and you will understand that you need only lessen and corrupt Christianity to hurl into the world half-truths and maddened virtues, as Chesterton says, which once kissed but will now for ever hate each other. That is why the modern world abounds in debased analogies of Catholic mysticism and shreds of laicized Christianity.

15. Consider the Rousseauist dogma of natural Goodness. With Jean-Jacques it is, I am fully aware, only an abyss of contradictions and ambiguities.[68] The wretched "thinker" loses himself in the different sense of the word *nature*, jumbling together the metaphysical essence of the human species, the individuality of each of us,* and the unfallen nature of Adam in the earthly paradise, besides mistaking the very nature of man, the essential characteristics of which are for him feeling and compassion, not reason. Yet this dogma

---

* In a sense Rousseau's whole mistake comes from the fact that when, rightly enough, he looks for the basic propensities of man, as being good, he wrongly seeks them in *sensitive individuality* and not in *essence* : instead of finding the first tendencies of natural morality he hits upon concupiscence itself.

has a very precise *practical* significance for him; it is, that to attain the good, we must beware of restraint or effort*—and it is not impossible to find its theoretical significance.

It means that man originally lived in a *purely natural* paradise of happiness and goodness, and that Nature herself will in future perform the function which grace fulfilled in the Catholic conception. It also means that such a state of happiness and goodness, of exemption from servile work and suffering, is *natural* to man, that is to say, essentially required by our nature. Not only, then, is there no original sin† of which we bear the guilt at our birth and still keep the wounds, not only is there in us no seat of concupiscence and unhealthy proclivities to incline us to evil, but, further, the state of suffering and hardship is one essentially *opposed to nature* and started by civilization, and our nature demands that we should, at any cost, be freed from it. That is what the dogma of natural Goodness amounts to.

But whence comes this anti-Christian dogma? If it is linked with the philosophical myth of Nature,‡ yet it is something quite different from the hedonistic thesis of a Diderot. With Jean-Jacques it only follows the set lines of an old theological truth. It is only a cutting down of the Christian dogma of adamic Innocence to fit the scheme of romantic naturalism.[70]

And certainly this venerable truth of primitive Goodness—the first to strengthen poor humanity when rightly understood[71]—is also the most treacherous and

---

* Ah! Let us not spoil man: he will always be good without difficulty. . . . *Émile*, Book 4 (Profession of Faith).

† Rousseau calls the dogma of original sin "a blasphemy." Letter to M. de Beaumont, 3, 67. (ed. Hachette.)

‡ See above, pp. 126–127.

dangerous. Jean-Jacques is not the first to draw extrav-
agant conclusions from it. You could find forerunners
in certain Christian sects of the Middle Ages. Nay
more, almost two thousand years before him, in
213 B.C., when Tsin-Cheu-Hoang ordered that all
books should be burnt, and had men of letters who tried
to prevent their destruction cruelly tortured, was it
not, as certain commentators say, because he had read
in Confucius and Mencius the same leading truth that
man was originally good, and had deduced from that,
like a premature enlightened Rousseauist despot, that
learning and civilization are the cause of the corruption of the people? But Rousseau had all Christian
wisdom behind him, and his fall was all the greater.

Consider again the Rousseauist dogma of Equality.
That too recalls a *naturalized* Gospel. There is a kind
of divine egalitarianism in the Gospel—the only true
egalitarianism, that divine freedom of omnipotent
Love, in Whose sight human greatness and littleness
are of no account—because every created thing is
equally naught before God—and Who establishes
among us a higher hierarchy independent of all our
inequalities. Positions are reversed, the humble are
exalted, men are assumed into the ranks of the Angels,
"*filii resurrectionis erunt aequales angelis in coelis*"—but all
through grace, and in the supernatural order, without
doing any hurt to the order and hierarchies of nature.
If now the shadow of this Gospel egalitarianism be
transferred to *the natural order*, then instead of the
assertion of the equal dependence of all in relation to
one same Master, a transcendent God sovereignly free,
we shall have an equal claim to independence formulated by all in the name of the immanent god of

Nature, and that sublime contempt for natural and rational subordinations and hierarchies, all equally levelled before an idol of Justice, which is the soul of democratic egalitarianism. "I do not like *curés*," said Louis-Philippe, "because they sing *deposuit de sede*." Jean-Jacques, a lackey of genius, turns the universe topsy-turvy in order to obtain his position as one of the predestined; Benedict Labre, by winning his, strengthens the order of the world.

Consider finally the Myth of the Revolution. Does not that, too, come from a *naturalization* of Christianity? To expect the resurrection of the dead and the universal judgement which will bring the kingdom of justice on earth as in heaven, to expect the revelation of the perfect Jerusalem where all is light, order, and joy: but to expect all this in the very conditions of the present life and expect it from the strength of man, not the grace of Christ; to believe that we are called to lead a divine life, the very life of God—"*ego dixi : dii estis*" —but to believe it of our natural life, not our life of grace; to proclaim the law of love of our neighbour, but in separation from the law of the love of God, and so to lower love, strong as death and stern as hell, to the level of what is most stupid and cowardly in the world, to the level of humanitarianism; to understand that there is in this world something awry, something horrible which ought not to be, but without seeing that the old Adam still falls, and the new Adam is still raised on the Cross and drawing souls to Him; and to want to have the world restored by man's power or the effort of nature and not helped and supported by the diligent humility of the virtues and by the divine medicines dispensed by the Bride of Christ, until

the Bridegroom Himself shall come with fire and make
all things new: in a word, to laicize the Gospel, to
keep the human aspirations of Christianity but do
away with Christ—is not all this the whole essence of
the Revolution?

16. It was Jean-Jacques who completed that amazing
performance, which Luther began, of inventing a
Christianity separate from the Church of Christ: it
was he who completed the *naturalization* of the Gospel.
It is to him that we owe that corpse of Christian ideas
whose immense putrefaction poisons the universe
to-day. Rousseauism is "a Christian heresy of mystical
type," says M. Seillière. A heresy, fundamentally and
radically, I grant; a complete realization of the Pela-
gian heresy through the mysticism of sensation; let
us say more exactly that Rousseauism is a radical
naturalistic corruption of Christian feeling.

That very fact, it seems to me, shows us how useful
the study of Jean-Jacques Rousseau is for us. It provides
us with a certain principle of discrimination. If we
discover in ourselves, if we meet in the world, any
principle that depends on Rousseauism, we shall know
that this principle is not a new one, a young principle
that we might be tempted to adopt and christianize,
but that it is an old principle working itself out, that it
is Christianity liquefying and rotten; and we shall
throw it out, for there is nothing more absurd than to
try to join and harmonize a living form and its corruption.

We must, then, realize that the Church alone can
keep in its purity the Gospel leaven which the careful
woman hides in three measures of meal and which
makes the whole paste rise. Everyone else corrupts it

by handling it unwisely, and it is a terrible thing to handle unwisely the powers of a divine leaven.

Christ cannot be separated from His Church. Only in the Church is Christianity a living thing; outside her it dies, and begins to dissolve, like every corpse. If the world does not live by the living Christianity in the Church, it dies of the corrupted Christianity outside the Church. In no way can the world avoid it and be rid of it. The more the human race denies its King, the more firmly He holds it.

17. An examination of Rousseau's religious conceptions allows us to discover very suggestive filiations. It is not without use to trace out the doctrines, or at least the tendencies, which can with good right invoke his patronage.

It is well known that, according to him, "the state of reflection is an unnatural state. The man who meditates is a corrupted animal";* "general and abstract ideas are the source of the greatest errors of men, never did metaphysical jargon lead to the discovery of a single truth";† "reasoning, far from enlightening us, blinds us; it does not raise our soul, it enervates and corrupts the judgement, which it should perfect."‡ In that universal suspicion which falls on "the art of reasoning," the heart alone "is called as a witness." "Provided that you *feel* that I am right, I do not bother to prove it to you."§ And lastly,

* *Discours sur l'origine de l'inégalité.*
† *Émile,* Book IV (Profession of Faith).
‡ Second letter to Sophie. Unpublished works and correspondence, ed. Streckeisen—Moulton, 1861. (Masson, II, p. 55.)
§ Second letter to Sophie (Masson II, p. 56). Rousseau goes on thus (2nd and 4th letters): "I want to speak to your heart and I do not attempt to argue with philosophers. It is no good their proving to me that they are right; I feel they are lying and I am convinced that

a celebrated text the true sense of which is shown by
the foregoing passages: "I shall never reason about
the nature of God unless I am forced to do so by the
feeling of His relations with me. My son, keep your
soul ever desirous that there should be a God and
you will never doubt it." This formula is not without
truth in reference to the dispositions of the subject—
to what we call material causality and the "remotio
prohibentium." But Jean-Jacques means that it is
the only formal means of having a real firm assurance
of the existence of God.[72]

So then his only criterion is in fact the connivances
of desire, affective connaturality, the peremptory
emotions of feeling. Otherwise stated, it is by what he
wants and not by what is, it is *per ordinem ad appetitum*
that he judges truth. "The truth which I know," he
wrote to Dom Deschamps, "or what I take to be it, is
very *lovable*."* Alas, even in his case the intelligence
renounces its essential demands with such difficulty
that, in spite of all, it cannot fail to perceive the inadequacy of such a motive. Hence that peculiar reserve
of doubt which Rousseau, like Kant, has always in the
background of his philosophic faith. When he sees
it too clearly, he falls back on the theory of consoling
illusions. "Even if the limitless Being with Whom the
heart is busied did not exist, it would still be good for
the heart to be constantly busied with Him, to have

---

they feel it too. . . . If you feel that I am right, I ask no more than
that." cf. 2nd letter to Sophie: "In philosophy, substance, soul, body,
eternity, movement, liberty, necessity, contingency, etc., are so many
words which one is forced to use every moment and no one has ever
understood. . . ." So far as he is concerned that is true enough.
Émile, Book IV (Profession of Faith).
* Masson, II, 261, 25 June, 1761.

more self-control, and be stronger, happier, and wiser."* "I want to live as an honest man and a good Christian," he said to Mme. d'Épinay, "because I want to die in peace, and because moreover this feeling does not disturb the course of my life in any way and because it makes me form a hope that is sweet to me, when I shall be no more. . . . It is perhaps an illusion; but if I had a more consoling illusion I should adopt that."†

This theory of consoling illusions which may excusably be thought absurd, is difficult to avoid with a psychology like Jean-Jacques's. "He never pierced that heaven of truth which disconcerts and frightens. . . . What he cares about is not so much the objectivity of his faith as the comforting certainty he finds in it."‡ When such a man seriously sets his heart in the dreams and chimeras he enjoys in imagination,[73] and when in his eyes "there is nothing beautiful but what is not," a thoroughly pleasant fiction cannot but have more value and at last come to have for him hardly less practical certainty than the things he knows to be true. If we want a label, we may say that Jean-Jacques, like Luther, is a very perfect and unalloyed specimen of *anti-intellectualist* religious thought.

He is also a *pragmatist*,[74] I mean in feeling and tendency (I would not on that account saddle him with the theories of contemporary pragmatists). The "truths of practice" are the only ones which have any interest

* *Nouvelle Héloïse*, part 3, letter 18. cf. part 6, letter 8: "I would give my life," said Julie, speaking of M. de Wolmar, "to see him convinced; if it is not for his happiness in the other world, it is for his happiness in this."
† *Mémoires de Madame d'Épinay*, II, 394–395. Masson, I, 185.
‡ Masson, II, 261, 266.

for him. In other words, he does not desire truth for its own sake (rather would he fear it, he would be afraid of finding it *cold*), he only desires it for the sake of the good of man and what gives value to human life. "The truth he loves is not so much metaphysical as moral."*

I can hardly refrain from observing here that he expresses himself just like William James. "I believe then that the world is governed by a mighty and wise will: I see it, or rather I feel it, and that is of conse-quence to me. But is this world eternal, or created? Is there a single source of things? Are there two, or several, and what is their nature? Of that I know nothing; and what does it matter to me? I renounce idle questions, which may disturb my self-respect, but are of no value to my conduct and are beyond my reason."† And again: "I only seek to know what concerns my conduct. As to dogmas, which influence neither actions nor morality, and which so many people worry about, I do not trouble about them at all."‡

Finally, Jean-Jacques is already definitely *immanent-ist*,—this word again I mean in its most general sense, and as expressing a fundamental tendency rather than any particular system. According to him, God can only manifest Himself to man by a spontaneous demand of nature, by a need of feeling, by an immediate experience.

So too the objective revelation of a supernatural truth and dogmatic faith are nothing to him. "Is it simple, is it natural," he asks, "that God should have

* Letter to Dom Deschamps, 25 June, 1761.
† Ibid.
‡ *Émile*, Book IV (Profession of Faith).

gone to look for Moses in order to speak to Jean-Jacques Rousseau?"*

This anti-rationalist, steeped (and inevitably, for he had nothing but feeling to set against them) in the sophisms of the false reason which he professes to despise, rejects the mysteries of the faith as being "not at all mysterious things," but "clear and palpable absurdities, things evidently false."† "I even confess," he writes in a letter in which he is defending the religious sense and the Christianity of nature, "that all formulas in matters of faith seem to me only so many chains of iniquity, falsehood and tyranny."‡

As to moral conduct, each man's conscience is absolutely self-sufficing, and needs no help, nor any teaching human or divine to enlighten and correct it. All *heteronomy* is excluded. Conscience is not only the proximate rule of our free determinations against which it is never allowable to act; it is also infallible, an immediate revelation of the divine oracles, springing from the very ground of our heart. "I would rather trust to this inward and incorruptible judge who passes nothing bad and condemns nothing good and never deceives when consulted in good faith."§ It has been pointed out that this "divine instinct," this "infallible judge of good and evil which makes men like God," had been very devoutly consulted by Jean-Jacques when he was abandoning his children. He had not failed to "scrutinize" the thing "by the laws of nature, justice, and reason, and by those of that pure holy

---

* Letter to M. de Beaumont.
† Letter to d'Alembert.
‡ Letter to M. X. . . . ., of Bourgoin, 15 January, 1769.
§ Letter to M. Perdriau, 28 September, 1754 (Corresp. générale de J.-J. R., ed. par Théophile Dufour, vol. II, p. 134).

religion, eternal as its author, which men have soiled, etc." "That arrangement," adds the man of Nature, "appeared to me so good, so sensible, so *legitimate. . . .*" "If I was wrong in my results, nothing is more amazing than the security of soul with which I gave myself up to it."* "I well know," Diderot said to him, "that whatever you do, you will always have the witness of your conscience."

Can Jean-Jacques' piety need the help of a transcendent God? The Savoyard curate "talks" with God but "does not pray to Him." "I do not ask of Him . . . the power to do right: why ask Him for what He has given me?" Or else when Rousseau prays, it is "as the angels who praise God around His throne,"† it is to say: "Thy will be done," unless it be to cry, as M. Masson, who sees in such a formula the characteristic prayer of Jean-Jacques, says: "O God, come to me, speak to me, console me, and deserve that I proclaim Thee."[75]

Understand above all what is the last end of man in the Rousseauist religion. To become one with God, no doubt. But not by being raised by God to a participation in His life, rooted in Him by the vision of His essence. On the contrary, it is by absorbing, assimilating the Divinity in ourselves. Self, self, divine self, always self, it is always in himself that Jean-Jacques would have beatitude: "supreme enjoyment is in satisfaction with oneself. It is to merit this satisfaction that we are set on earth and endowed with liberty."[76] "Happiness on earth depends on the degree in which we withdraw from things and draw closer *to ourselves :*

* *Confessions*, book 8.
† 3rd Lettre de la Montagne.

we are then sustained by our own substance, but it is never exhausted."* "No, God of my soul, I will never upbraid You for having made it in Your image to the end that I may be *free, good, and happy, like You.*"†

Beatitude, in fact, is to be like God, enjoying "nothing *save Himself* and His own existence," in a state in which one is self-sufficient, like God."‡

"In Jean-Jacques' paradise," M. Masson well writes,§ "God Himself will discreetly vanish to leave room for Jean-Jacques. The paradise which he dreams is one which he will fill completely, one which will give him the highest pleasures in satisfaction with and enjoyment of himself, because he will feel that he is God Himself, free, good, and happy like Him. 'I long,' he says, 'for the moment when, freed from the shackles of the body, I shall be myself without contradiction, without division, and shall need only myself to be happy.'" Here we are certainly at the centre of Jean-Jacques's madness; but we are also at the heart of the Paradise of Immanence.

18. And yet, with all that, and while he denies original sin and redemption, Rousseau believes in the Gospel and calls himself a Christian. More, he directs consciences, he reinvigorates the salt of the earth, he calms restless abbés and troubled seminarists who go to him in their doubts. "What?" he wrote to one. "You would refuse to embrace the noble profession of

---

* Letter to Henriette (de Maugin?) 4 November, 1764 (Masson, II, p. 228). cf. Rêveries, 2e Promenade: "Little by little I accustomed myself to feeding my heart on its own substance, and finding all its nourishment within myself."

† *Émile*, Book 4 (Profession of Faith).

‡ *Rêveries*, 5e Promenade. cf. Masson, II, p. 230.

§ Masson: la Religion de Rousseau, Vol. II, ch. 3, p. 120.
Émile, Book 4 (Profession of Faith).

officer of morality? And that for a few puzzles of which neither „you nor I understand anything. You have only to take them and give them for what they are worth, quietly bringing Christianity back to its true object."* And that is what he sets himself to do, that Savoyard curate who, having rejected the faith, re-remains conscientiously in the Church, and continues to exercise his ministry in it as before—nay, better than before. "Formerly I said Mass with the carelessness with which one ultimately does the most serious things when one does them too often; with my new principles, I celebrate it with more veneration; I am penetrated with the majesty of the Supreme Being, etc."†

We well know that tone, and it has often been pointed out that the Savoyard curate is the first Modernist priest. But whence comes this modernism of Rousseau's, what are its immediate origins? It comes from les Charmettes and Mme. de Warens. M. Seillière has rightly stressed the importance of the transmission to Jean-Jacques, by the attentions of his dear *mamma*, of a quietism debased enough since Mme. Guyon's time. There we have weakness of false mysticism which is exceedingly curious. Jean-Jacques was formed in Mme. de Warens' spiritual atmosphere; he was stamped with it for ever. Pietist when she was Protestant, quietist after her conversion, the kind-hearted lady, in her strong conviction of the indifference of external acts, was not content with initiating Jean-Jacques and Claude Anet, the gardener, into the blessings of sexual communism; she initiated Jean-

---

* Letter to the Abbé de Carondelet, 6 January, 1764.
† The disciples of the Savoyard curate will communicate and fulfil their Easter duties in the same sentiments of "respect without faith." Masson, III, 62–63.

F

Jacques at the same time into the life of the spirit. She was his "theological deliverer."* It is essential to bring out this meeting of Rousseau, at a decisive moment of his moral evolution, with a depraved spirituality. It would seem that if we always find a mystical touch at the beginning of divine works, a touch of false mysticism is always encountered at the beginning of the great works of disorder. It was with Mme. de Warens that Jean-Jacques developed his naturalistic religiosity, bewitching himself in his morning walks in the orchard of les Charmettes with his *feeling of virtue* and his vague emotions, and his effusions before the author of *pleasant nature*.†

There did he learn those strange collusions of the carnal and the divine in which he always delighted, and that care to heighten by sin the savour of innocence,[77] in a sort of mockery of St. Paul's saying, *"virtus in infirmitate perficitur."* It was from Mme. de Warens that he learnt no longer to fear Hell or believe original sin, which gives the lie too frankly to his heart, which *feels* that it is naturally good.‡ Let us listen to him, his deadly sweetness is instructive. He explains that Mme. de Warens did not believe in Hell. You must be wicked to believe in it. "Devout people, spiteful and bilious, see nothing but Hell because they would like to damn the whole world. Loving and gentle souls hardly ever believe in it; and one of the things which always amazes me is to see the good Fénelon speak of it in his *Télémaque* as if he seriously believed in it. But I hope he was lying then, for after

---

* Cf. *Confessions*, Book 6, Masson, Vol. I, p. 68.
† *Confessions*, ibid.
‡ "Man is naturally good, as I believe and have the happiness to feel." *Answer to Bordes*, note.

all, however truthful you may be, you must lie sometimes when you are a bishop. Mamma did not lie to
me; and that soul without bitterness, who could not
imagine a vindictive and angry God, saw only clemency
and mercy where the devout see nothing but justice
and punishment." Rousseau remarks thereupon that
the doctrine of original sin and redemption is destroyed
by this system, and the "foundation of common
Christianity," as he calls it, is shaken by it, and that
Catholicism cannot continue. "Yet mamma too,"
he adds, "was a good Catholic, or said she was, and
she certainly said so in very good faith. It seemed to
her that the Scriptures were explained too literally and
too harshly. All that we read in them about eternal
torments seemed to her merely intended to terrify or
figurative. In a word, faithful to the religion she had
embraced, she admitted sincerely its whole profession
of faith; but when it came to discussion of each article,
it turned out that she believed quite differently from
the Church, whilst at the same time submitting to it."*

An admirable formula of the modernist state of
mind! Recommended to ecclesiastics embarrassed by
the oath of Pius X. But that is the state of mind of
Mme. de Warens. If Jean-Jacques is the father of
modernism, Mme. de Warens is deservedly its *mamma*.

Jean-Jacques, let us add, is not accustomed to care
for his offspring himself, and his paternities are a burden to him. He did not intend to be the father of the
Revolution, for despite the demagogic sentiments which
he affected at the time of his *Discours* and his friendship
with Diderot, his secret leanings were for peace and
social preservation, expedient for the calm of his

* *Confessions*, Book 6.

dreaming. Nor is he deliberately the father of modernism, I mean of the religious ideas prepared by Leibnitz and Lessing and specially adapted to the difficulties of Protestant theology, which, planted by him in Catholic soil, have ended in modernism after a long period of development. These tendencies come, in him, from an effort to defend the religious and Christian conception of life against the negative spirit of the philosophers—by entirely dispensing with reason, which was indeed very weak in him, and the assistance of grace, which could find no way into a man so occupied by self. Then he had nothing left on which to ground religion and renew Christianity but the requirements of feeling; and if such a religion and such a Christianity thus grounded and renewed were to flow into the Catholic mould, they were bound there to turn into modernism.

As Jean-Jacques himself saw very well, *he felt that the philosophers were lying, but was unable to prove it.* And that revolt of instinct against false reason was not bad in itself, for, after all, if Jean-Jacques's intellect was not physically qualified for philosophy, that was not his fault, nor a reason for yielding to Voltaire. The misfortune is that, instead of refraining from philosophizing, since he was not capable of it, he would philosophize on all occasions and try to save everything by himself, and repair solely out of his own resources the ravages of false reason. When reason is too deeply impaired by error it most certainly could not recover unaided; it must have the *gratia sanans*. But only sound reason can truly repair the ravages of false reason. Nothing beneath reason can do it.

We must grant M. Pierre-Maurice Masson that

Rousseau stimulated a wide return to religious feeling —but to what religious feeling? Doubtless the hearts which the intuitive philosophy caused to perish of inanition were profoundly stirred by him, doubtless many "weak" souls like his own may have been helped, against atheism and in the desire of moral good, by the same means which had helped him. And our nature is so feeble, so illogical, so unstable, so mixed, it provides such unforeseen turns; it is besides so probable that the moral mimesis of Jean-Jacques may have awakened in his disciples—less abnormal than he— truly healthy longings and true stirrings of conscience; finally, grace is so skilful to profit by the least signs of moral life in order to take root and sprout in us, that in fact Rousseau may well have had over many the kind of influence which M. Masson attributes to him. But that is only part of his influence, and the least important and most occasional part. On the general movement of modern thought that influence has been quite different. If it has prevented certain bruised reeds from breaking completely, it has bruised and spoiled internally an immense multitude of other thinking reeds. If it has—for the time—preserved among men a few parts of truth, it has been by debasing truth to make it acceptable to them, and that is the great sin. Much less vile and much less despicable personally than Voltaire, whom he had the merit of *hating*, Rousseau, in reality, is a thousand times worse than Voltaire because he provided men no longer with a mere negation, but with a religion outside the indivisible Truth. He only *kept up Catholic feeling* in the *élite* of French intellectuals by perverting it; and it is only by accident, *materialiter*, that he prepared the Catholic renaissance of the time of Chateaubriand (although I confess that it owes many weaknesses to him). By nature he himself tends directly to an abominable sentimentality, to a devilish parody of Christianity, the decomposition of Christianity and all the sicknesses and apostasies which follow; and to them he leads modern thought.

19. Let us not be mistaken about Rousseau's optimism and naturalism. Refuse of the supernatural order, says the latter; the goodness of Nature, says the former—that is, the goodness of the secret principle immanent in our nature to whose movements the sincere heart abandons itself. Yes, in this sense we do find both in Rousseau. But this optimism is more burdened with despair and more Manichæan than the bitterness of a Schopenhauer, for it condemns everything that is, it hates existence. What it pronounces good is not, in fact, real nature, the work of God with all its measures and all its laws; it is a dream nature which the individual carries hidden in the folds of his singularity, the nature which only blossoms fully in "our inhabitants" and protests against real nature.

And this naturalism or "naturism" is not only anti-social, it is also anti-physical. It regards as falsehood and sacrilege, not only the restraints of society and the subordination of the individual to the common good of the family and city, but primarily and more fundamentally the restraints of specific nature and the subordination of the individual to the good of the species. The private world of each one of us, his sensitive individuality, is that not a divine Person? Thus does Jean-Jacques carry to its highest degree the old Lutheran conflict between Gospel and Decalogue.[78]

now the conflict between the immanent Morality and the external Law. Kant's whole endeavour was to find a solution for this conflict, keeping in the line of Luther and Rousseau. The autonomous and law-giving will; the noumenal man, author of the law which the empirical man obeys; of this laborious ephemeral system there is left only a more cruel claim to illusory liberty and a homicidal adoration of man.

Luther and Rousseau, as theorists, do not preach the liberty of the flesh. They profess to belong to the spirit (and would they have had any effect without that?). Logic embarrasses neither of them. Luther intends that faith-trust, although justifying without works a nature which remains fundamentally depraved, should yet be crowned with a superstructure of good works. And he grieved to see that graceful super-structure fall through the malice of the devil as the true Gospel spread amongst men. Rousseau likewise intends that holy Nature, rediscovered by pure souls in their inmost selves and good without virtue, should yet produce virtuous works by spontaneous flowering, and he curses sincerely the "repulsive" sensualist "maxims" of a Diderot. These reformers preach evil? Nonsense! Their intentions are good; they only leave out reality, divine and human.

The fundamental question for man is, in the practical order, to find the conditions of liberty. Jean-Jacques saw that with a vengeance; but he answered all awry. Man is not born free,* he becomes free; and he only gains his liberty on condition that he serves. Do you

---

* It is obvious that we are not here speaking of free will, an essential property of the human being. We are speaking of liberty in the sense of absence of restraint.

think we do not know that the law holds in slavery the man who suffers its restraint? That state of slavery is our natural state. As for the saints, they were free, and they have taught us the secret of the state of liberty, which is supernatural. Love is that secret.

Because we are not essentially good, we only bear fruit if we are pruned. But because we are grafted on to the only Son, on to the divine Truth in person, we are branches who are sons, and the hand that prunes us is the hand of love. *"Pater meus agricola est."* It is when love is consummated that liberty is won. Love, which is the beloved present in the lover as the weight which draws him—*amor meus pondus meum*,—is the deepest personal instinct of him who loves. He who acts from love acts without constraint, for love drives away fear. Sanctity, fulfilling the law out of love, is no longer under restraint to the law. There is only one liberty, that of the saints.

Christian wisdom has not avoided the problem of liberty, it has attacked it boldly along its whole line. That wisdom must end a book of which this problem really forms the chief subject.

"We must consider that the sons of God are led by the Spirit of God not like slaves but like free men. For we call him free who is "his own cause" and therefore that which we do freely is what we do of ourselves (*ex nobis ipsis*), and that is what we do of our own will. But what we do against our will, we do as slaves, not as free persons, whether an absolute compulsion be laid upon us, or compulsion be mingled with what is voluntary, as when a man wills to do or suffer what is less against his will that he may escape what is more against it. Well, then, in that He infuses the love

of God into us, the Spirit of holiness inclines us to act
by making us act according to the very force of our own
will. (For it is the quality of affection that the lover
be at one with his beloved in the things which he
wills.) The sons of God are, therefore, led freely by the
Spirit of God, out of love, not slavishly out of fear.
'You have not received a spirit of bondage to be yet
in fear, but a spirit of adoption whereby we cry
Abba! Father!'

"Now since the will is of its nature ordered to what
is truly good, when, under the influence of a passion, a
vice, or a bad disposition, a man turns away from what
is truly good, that man, *if we consider the essential
order of the will*, acts as a slave, since he allows himself to be inclined against that order by some extraneous
cause. But if we consider the act of the will *as it is then
inclined towards a seeming good*, then he acts freely when he
follows his passion or corrupt disposition, and he acts
as a slave if, his will being still so inclined, he abstains
from what he wills out of fear of the law which forbids it.

"But the Holy Spirit inclines the will towards the
true good by love; by love He causes the will to lean
wholly towards that very thing which is in line with its
deepest desire. And so He takes away at once that
double slavery [that double *heteronomy* in modern jargon],
the slavery by which man, the slave of passion and sin,
acts against the natural ordination of his will; and the
slavery by which, the slave, and not the lover of the
law, he acts according to the law against the movement
of his will. 'Where the Spirit of the Lord is,' says the
Apostle Paul, 'there is liberty'; and 'If you are
led by the Spirit, you are no longer under the law.'"*

* St. Thomas: *Summa contra Gentiles*, IV, 22.

When we have thus become friends of God by the grace of Christ, love makes us free. "A great thing is love. Love is born of God and cannot rest but in God. He who loves has wings, he rejoices, he is free, nothing holds him. He gives all for all and possesses all in all, because he rests above all things in that supreme unity whence all good flows and proceeds. To love, nothing is burdensome, nothing impossible. Love thinks it may and can do all things. Therefore it is able to do all things. Love is circumspect, humble, and upright; not soft, nor light, not busied in vain things; it is sober, chaste, abiding, calm, and watchful over all the senses. Love watches, and sleeping, slumbers not. In weariness it is not tired, in distress it is not disquieted, in fear it is not troubled. It is swift, sincere, pious, pleasant, and joyful; strong, patient, faithful, prudent, steadfast, and constant, and never seeks itself. . . ."*

It is heartbreaking to see so many intelligent creatures looking for liberty apart from truth and apart from love. Needs must they then seek it in destruction; and they will not find it. And all over the earth the mystics and saints bear witness to the love which gives liberty. The deliverance for which all men long is only gained at the end of the way of the spirit, when love—a measureless love, for "the measure of loving God is to love Him without measure"†—has made the creature one spirit with God.

---

* *Imitation*, III, 5.
† St. Bernard: *De diligendo Deo.*

NOTES

SOME ABBREVIATIONS USED IN NOTES

Weim.: Weimer Edition (*Kritisch Gesamtausgabe* 1883—
in course of publication).

Erl.: Erlangen Edition *Sämtliche Werke* (1826–1857)—
67 8vo. vols.

Enders: *Dr. Martin Luthers Briefwechsel* (Kalw and Stuttgart
1884).

Corpus Reformatorum: Melanchthon, "*Historia de vita
et actis Lutheri*" (Wittenberg 1545).

NOTES

LUTHER

1. "I was a pious monk, attached to my Order; so much so that I dare to say: if ever monk entered heaven by his monkery, I can enter it too." Erl., 31, 173.

2. Not to mention spiritual influences which might exasperate that state of anguish, it seems difficult to dismiss here the hypothesis of a neuropathic disorder. Cochlaeus relates that one day, at Mass, whilst the priest was reading the Gospel of the dumb demoniac, Luther was seized with terror and cried out suddenly: "Ha! non sum! non sum!" and fell full length on the floor of the church, thrown down as if by a thunderbolt. (Félix Kuhn: *Luther, sa vie et son œuvre*, I, p. 55.)

3. "*Were it not that I am a doctor*," he wrote later, "the devil would often have slain me with this argument: You have no authority!" Walch, *Luther's Werke*, XXII, 1035–1036. Otto Scheel has shown[1] that Luther's study of scholasticism was deeper than Denifle had thought. Nevertheless it was a scholasticism corrupted by Occam and Gabriel and by the nominalist "pragmatic" spirit which the routine of the School develops too naturally— a spirit bent upon practical application, controversial success or "donnish" facility rather than truth.

4. It was intentionally that we wrote "in fact" and "in the highest and most subtle order," that is to say in

[1] *Martin Luther, von Katholizismus zur Reformation I*, Auf der Schule und Universität, 1916.

the order of mystical experience and of the spiritual life, in the relations between the soul and God and of the interior search for Christian perfection. This mystical "egocentrism," an illusion of the interior life, is quite other than a theoretical affirmation declaring man more interesting than God. That is why all the texts in which Luther reproduces the traditional teaching on the subordination of man to God are quite beside the point: even where he professes a kind of doctrine of pure love of God (or rather a pure hate of ourselves)—writing for example that we should wish to be damned, on account of our sinfulness (*ideo oportet . . . optare nos perdi et damnari*), in short, offer ourselves to hell, without which we shall not be forgiven.[1] It is in his doctrine of justification (vide p. 15) as in the preponderance of the problem of redemption in his theology that one finds, not a direct expression but a change in phrase and idea, and an indirect sign of unconscious "egocentrism" of a wholly spiritual and mystical order, which is for us the first principle of Luther's religious and psychological evolution.

And to avoid all misunderstanding let us explain once more: It is not *theoretically and according to Luther*, but *actually and according to Truth* that the Lutheran doctrine of justification, by denying that sanctifying grace washes away original sin and makes us intrinsically good, shuts us forever within ourselves (vide p. 15) and makes man, not God, the centre of our religious life: for since we are made no longer sharers in the divine nature, we can produce no vital act of our own, no essentially personal act which comes from God vivifying us supernaturally.

5. "I was then the most presumptuous of the claimants to justice, *praesumptuosissimus justitiarius*." (quoted by Janssen: *L'Allemagne et la Réforme*, Paris, Plon, II, 71). "Relying on my works, I trusted not in God, but in my own justice. I looked to climb into heaven." (Kuhn, I, 55) (cf. Erl., 19, 419; Op. Exeg. lat., V. 267; VII,

[1] Comment. on the Ep. to the Rom. Ficker II, 220; cf. ibid. 205, 215, 217–220.

72-73.) Denifle has shown that he greatly exaggerated the austerities of his convent, which followed a very moderate rule; but he does seem to have thrown himself, on his own account, into those violent and presumptuous penances which make bad monks. "I became the persecutor and horrible torturer of my own life: I fasted, I watched, I wore myself out in prayer, which is nothing but suicide." (Janssen, II, 71.) The reactions were sometimes peculiar. "I have such an aversion for Christ that when I saw one of His images, for example the Crucifix, I at once felt terrified; I would more willingly have seen the devil." (Janssen, II, 72). "My spirit was broken and I was always sad . . ." (Erl., 31, 273.) The brethren had no understanding of these sadnesses, and thought that he wanted to make an impression by his singularity, or that he was possessed by the devil. (Kuhn, I, 54.)

6. Enders I, 66–67. It is self-evident that the responsibility for the state of affairs which is denounced in the letter quoted falls as much upon the *régime* of the Augustinians of Wittenberg and on Luther's religious superior as upon himself. Denifle has, moreover, explicitly said this (Fr. trans. 2cd. ed, I, 62). On the meaning of the passage concerning the breviary and the Mass, M. Karl Holl (Rev. de théol. et de phil., Lausanne, Aug-Dec. 1927) states that Denifle has been "vigorously reprimanded" by M. A. V. Müller who "as a former Dominican is informed on those questions." These rebukes of M. Müller[1] have been severely criticized in their turn by M. Paquier, the translator of the French version of Denifle (I, 389 sq.). "Raro mihi integrum tempus est horas persolvendi et celebrandi," means according to M. Müller, "There seldom is left to me time to say my office and celebrate Mass *recollectedly and with ease; with*

[1] Need one add that neither a Protestant writer animated by strong anti-Catholic prejudices, nor a Dominican who dedicates his book to his wife Lidia and his daughter Ada, seems specially qualified to appraise the fidelity of a monk to the breviary and the Mass?

great difficulty I manage to say my office and celebrate Mass." In fact Luther celebrated Mass every day; his words refer only to the headlong way in which he carried out his duties and to the distractions of which he humbly accused himself.

A fantastic explanation, remarks M. Paquier. It is in 1533 and 1538 that Luther declares that in the past he said Mass every day. These statements can therefore be tied down to a definite period; they can be true of the first years of priesthood and not of those which border on the final break. On the other hand Luther would say: "that in the years before 1520, when he completely gave up saying his office, he was in the habit of saying on Saturday the whole office for the past week,[1] but, he added, by the end his head was spinning. These words are too precise not to refer to actual facts."[2] One easily sees that they agree with the obvious meaning of the letter to Lange.

M. Karl Holl would have it that Luther was sad when he wrote the passage in question. Let us say rather that he was filled with *helpless regret*. In any case we do not quote this passage to show that Luther thenceforward had no affection in his heart for Mass and breviary. We quote it to establish a fact which none may contest, namely, that he was plunged into feverish activity, which left him no time to pray as he should have done, and to turn himself to God.[3]

---

[1] Zeitschrift für Kirchengeschichte, IV, 1886, p. 330, no. 22 (*Dicta Melanchthoniana*). See similar quotations in Grisar I, 225. In parenthesis one must not think that in the letter of Luther the word *persolvere* means to finish, *to say in entirety*. It means no more than *to say, to recite ;* Luther uses the word of the prayer *Aperi Domini* which precedes the recital of office: "Domine . . . has tibi horas persolvo" (M. Paquier's note).

[2] Denifle-Paquier, 2e. éd. I, 391.

[3] It may be remarked also, with Denifle, that although he often preached recourse to prayer, Luther himself "had never been a man of prayer" (Denifle-Paquier, I, 196), and that later he had nothing but scorn for the spiritual life and contemplation. (Ibid. III, 414-415. cf. *In Galat.* 1535. Weim., XL. ,P. II 110, 14-24.)

7. Sermon of the 16th January, 1519, Weimer, IX,
215, 13 (early draft not corrected by Luther). "It is a
horrible struggle," he says again (ibid., 4-6). "I have
known it well, and you must know it too, oh I know it
well, when the devil excites and inflames the flesh . ."

Later on Luther, while declaring in conformity with
his fundamental thesis, that the conjugal act is never accomplished without sin (Weim., X, P. II, 304, 6, 1522), and
that "God covers over the sin, without which there could
be no married people," (Opp. exeg. lat., IV, 10—c. 1538.
Weim., XLII, 582, 29-31) says even more clearly: "This
saying of God: 'Increase and multiply' is not a precept,
it is more than a precept, it is a divine work whose hinder-
ing or allowing does not lie in our power; for me it is as
necessary as my manhood, more necessary than eating,
drinking, evacuating, sleeping and waking.

"This work is of our very nature, an instinct as deeply
rooted as the organs through which it works" (Sermon on
Marriage, 1522. Weim., X, P. II, 276, 21-26). "God
does not take from man and woman their special fashion-
ing, sexual organs, seed and its fruits; a Christian's body
must generate, multiply and behave like those of other
men, like those of birds and all animals, he was created
by God for that, thus where God performs no miracle,
man must unite with woman and woman with man."
(1523, Weim., XII, 113. cf. XII, 66, 31). Here is a
significant example of the Reformer's way of thinking.
The moral precept, imposed upon *humanity* as a whole
to *preserve the species gifted with reason,* in order that the
number of the just may be filled at the end of time, is
confused with the natural pressure put upon each individual by his *animal* nature. Luther's thought is typical
of one aspect of modern thought, it materializes everything
it touches. This sermon on marriage provides a fit
entrance for the miseries of an age which hates chastity
no less than poverty.

8. Sometimes, as Grisar points out, this statement only
means with Luther that concupiscence, "the seat of sin,"

is *ineradicable*.[1] But from this perfectly exact sense Luther, because he identifies concupiscence with original sin thus become ineffaceable, and because he does not admit the possibility of an intrinsic justice in man, slips into the sense which Denifle has so stressed, and according to which concupiscence is *unconquerable, irresistible*, if not in each particular case, at least in general for the whole of our life. "When he says that concupiscence is absolutely invincible, Luther does not only mean to state that it never dies and that it is always reviving in us with its incitements to break the law, but moreover that it comes to us with the features of Antæus, the unconquerable giant whom no one resisted and who crushed all his adversaries." (Denifle: *Luther et le luthéranisme*, trad. J. Paquier, Paris, Picard, 2e. éd., 1916, II, 399) cf. *Commentary on the Epistle to the Romans* (Ficker, II, 145, 1): "Hic Cerberus, latretor incompescibilis, et Anthæus in terra dimissus insuperabilis."

As M. Paquier very rightly shows (Denifle, II, 391, note 1), the very doctrine of the absolute uselessness of good works logically presupposes this theory, for, after all, if works are useless it is because original sin had irremediably vitiated our nature and our activity proceeds from a radically corrupt source. When Karl Holl in order to defend Luther from Denifle, undertakes to show that for him *concupiscentia* is identical with self-love

[1] In theological language, the word concupiscence does not only mean the desires of the flesh but the general propensity towards an uncontrolled love of oneself and of perishable things. This propensity is the "seat of sin" (*fomes peccati*) which is in us even after Baptism, like a wound in our nature—it is the mark of original sin, but it is not that sin, which is washed away by Baptism and Sanctifying Grace.

When Luther says that *concupiscence is invincible* he is thinking of it in this universal sense, and not merely as the desires of the flesh. (Has not Denifle assimilated even more than Luther the two meanings of the word?) M. Karl Holl does not see that if Luther identifies concupiscence and self-love he still uses it in the general sense, the origin of revolt, and of sin, and in the more restricted sense of desires of the flesh. In any case M. Karl Holl admits that for Luther (Gesammelte Aufsätze zur Kirchengeschichte t. I, *Luther*, 1927, p. 136–137) concupiscence is much more than the "seat of sin," it is *sin* in the most strict and serious sense of the word.

which creeps in everywhere to corrupt our best intentions,[1] he confirms, in spite of himself, Denifle's interpretation. For if our nature is so vitiated that our natural desire for happiness is fundamentally poisoned by a culpable egoism and constitutes—under the name of concupiscence, and in us, as original sin—a *sin* pure and simple, it is clear that that sin is *invincible, unconquerable* and as impossible to escape as our own nature. We must then admit that Denifle here touched the heart of the question and that, despite the harshness which sometimes mars his analyses, he managed to penetrate Luther's psychology more skilfully than Grisar.[2] "We must besides hasten to add that Luther did not draw from his system all it logically contained"; (thus he often urges the struggle against bad tendencies, and he would have justification by faith crowned by the fulfilment of the commandments). "His nominalism, a certain good sense, the fear of compromising his cause, all combined to allow him these contradictions and dictate them." (Paquier, loc. cit.)

9. As the preceding pages show clearly enough, it is a *mystical*, spiritual fall that we are thinking of, and not a carnal fall (a thesis, all the more probable, in that it puts back the decisive crisis of Luther, see n. 10). On this point our interpretation differs substantially from

[1] Karl Holl, *Gesammelte Aufsätze zur Kirchengeschichte. I Luther* Tübingen, 1927, p. 130, 137, 181.

[2] This does not mean that we accept Denifle's thesis on Luther's crisis as it stands. For us, when Luther affirms the invincibility of concupiscence, it was his personal experience which was the first condition of his doctrinal "illumination" and which played the chief rôle, but it was not in the flesh or sexually that Luther was first beaten, it was spiritually and mystically.

Denifle is an eminent scholar, but frequently his explanations are material. The vigour with which he carries on his work of pulling down, if more favourable to psychological penetration than a certain formal liberalism, carries him on to excessive simplification; and the great speculative interest of certain of Luther's theological errors sometimes remains hidden from him. These observations do not lessen the importance of the work which opened up once more Lutheran studies. The philosopher must go to it particularly for *materials* which are, moreover, valuable.

that of Denifle. It was *after* this mystical fall that the
desires of the flesh arose. "I am here in idleness, alas,
neglecting prayer and not sighing once for the Church of
God," he was to write from Wartburg in 1521. "*I burn
with all the desires of my unconquered flesh.* It is ardour of
the spirit that I ought to feel; but it is the flesh, desire,
laziness, idleness, and sleepiness that possess me. . . . (to
Melanchthon, 13 July 1521, Enders III, 189). Even
allowing for a certain conventional exaggeration in these con-
fidences one cannot eliminate the confession they contain.

9A. It is in no way opposed to the psychological analysis here sketched out, that Luther regarded what happened
in the Tower, where he was made conscious of his doctrine
of grace, as an *immediate revelation* of God. Luther is not,
in our eyes, a man conquered by the flesh, who invents
afterwards a theoretical justification for his state. No!
For as it was in his search for ascetic and mystical perfection that his interior life had at first crumbled (because
he sought rather his own sanctity and the *feeling* that he
was without sin than to adhere to God through love) and
it was against a temptation, above all spiritual, that—on
account of this initial false position—he vainly struggled,
only to admit himself beaten in the end. Then, it is true,
one may say that he gave in to the flesh, but it is mystically,
at the bottom of his heart, by consenting with his mind
to the misery of the flesh that cannot be uprooted, and to
the uselessness of human effort. All these spiritual disturbances formed the psychological accompaniment, and
the fixed conditions of the *divine illumination* of the Tower,
which allowed him to admit himself a sinner without
despairing of salvation (but despairing of the efficacious
and sanctifying power of grace), and gave him, at any
rate theoretically, peace within, by teaching him that we
are justified by the merits of Christ as though a cloak were
to hide the sin which is in us. Since Luther's reflection
on this point began, according to Denifle, in 1515, and
even, according to Karl Holl, before 1511, there is no
reason for saying that this theology was *subsequent in time*

to his internal experience, but rather that they developed *simultaneously* to culminate at the same moment the one in the experience in the Tower, the other in the confession that the radical evil which vitiates our will, is unconquerable. And in saying that Luther's doctrine expresses above all his interior states, his spiritual adventures and his personal history (p. 10) and that the first is born of the second (p. 9), it is an ontological priority, a priority *of nature*, and determining value rather than a chronological priority, a priority *in time*, that we attribute to the one over the other.

10. Opp. exeg. lat., VII (1540-41), p. 74, (Weim., XXXIII, 537, 24). Denifle would put Luther's decisive crisis in 1515. Karl Holl believes that it occurred earlier, and he would place the "*évenèment de la tour*," where took place the illumination (about the justice of Christ which is imparted to us by faith alone) which set his mind free, in the second visit to Wittenberg and before the beginning of the *léçons* on the Psalter. Cf. André Tundt, *Le développement de la pensée réligieuse, de Luther jusqu'en 1517*. Paris 1906; Henri Strohl *L'évolution de Luther jusqu'en 1515*, Strasburg 1922; *L'épanouissement de la pensée réligieuse de Luther de 1515 à 1520*, 1924; Cristiani; *Du Luthéranisme au Protestantisme, évolution réligieuse de Luther de 1517–1528;* Karl Holl, op. cit. 1927.

11. The famous *pecca fortiter* is not, for Luther, an *exhortation to sin*, and it is clearly not in this sense that we quote it. Luther thought that good works, while useless for salvation, must necessarily follow saving faith,[1] like a sort of epiphenomenon, and that this faith, making the soul inseparable from God, would prevent bad works. In stating the formula in question in his celebrated letter to Melanchthon (Aug. 1st, 1521), he was giving a précis of all his ascetical and theological dialectic, of all his treatment for souls, and it is as such that we recall it.

[1] "If you believe, good works will follow necessarily upon your faith." Weim., XII, 559 (1523).

Remaining sinful to the marrow of our bones (in the sense that concupiscence or original sin, ever present, vitiates all our acts fundamentally, even those which are externally good) we are, nevertheless, saved by the imputation of the merits of Christ. The essential thing is to recognize that we are sinners, frankly despairing of ourselves, admitting that we are sinners *for good and all* ("Deus non facit salvos ficte peccatores") then confidence in the merits of our Saviour will save us *for good and all*. Then it is clear that if, as it happens in practice (in spite of the infallible results theoretically attributed to faith, and no doubt because our faith is too weak) we fall back into sin, we have only to cling more violently to faith and we shall be saved. The only cure for the essential misery of human nature is to have recourse to faith-confidence and to strengthen it. That is why the only really serious and fatal sin is lack of faith. Even if an actual sin is an occasion for us to recognize our essential corruption and of practising our faith, that sin is of more worth to us than any good acts and all virtuous efforts.[1] Sin courageously, then, unhappy man! And believe even more courageously; all will go well with you. It is precisely because this formula is the living expression of Luther's theological dialectic that it is important to us, and that it is right to dwell upon it. The Reformer's fatal mistake is in believing that salvation can be attained by *faith* alone (which can coexist with sin[2]) and by an external

---

[1] "Et ecce vitio affectus in illa [bona gratiae et merita] praesumentis fit ut facilius in peccatis sit sperare in Deum et *tutius* quam in meritis et bonis. Et sic . . . *periculosum* est hominem in multis gratiis et meritis usque ad mortem relinqui, quia vix discet in Deum sperare, nisi difficillime, imo sine spiritu nequaquam." *Opera Latina varii arg.* I, 239, 1516. The letter to Weber only gives a picturesque and dramatic illustration of this morbid theology.

[2] According to Catholic dogma faith can coexist with sin, it is then "infirm faith," faith without charity or sanctifying grace. (It is the same with regard to hope.) That is why the sinner who has lost sanctifying grace and charity, can pray and strive to his utmost to receive them again.

For Luther, too, faith can exist with sin, but in another sense: (a) in the sense that our nature *as such* remains essentially bad and accursed

imputation—and not by *charity* which regenerates and justifies man from within, makes him produce really good works, and forces him to struggle so as to preserve, acquire and fortify the Virtues.

Luther knew the reality of our sinfulness, he should have known, too, and known better, the reality of grace, of charity and of infused justice. That is the great truth which is still unknown to the defenders of Luther (cf. Karl Holl, op. cit. 234), like him, victims of an entirely psychological and empirical theology which blinds them to the greatest work of God's power. As if the weaknesses and the impurities which we still see in ourselves (but which are not mortal sins) prevented the reality of regeneration which rectifies us intrinsically in the very essence of our soul and in its facilities.—From then for Luther *"Sufficit quod agnovimus,"* etc., *see* further note 38.

12. It was really to others, and in particular to Melanchthon that Luther left the *rationalizing* of the new doctrine. As Dilthey has clearly shown, Melanchthon and his Aristotle, sugared with humanism, nominalism and pedagogy, played from this point of view—until the metaphysics of Suarez which were to have a great success in the German Universities[1]—a very important part in preparing modern German philosophy. But it is from the Reformer that, from the beginning, came all the life and energy of the new theology. He was the head, and his spirit, covered, more or less, in the ashes of university scholasticism, was always to lurk in the Protestant German conscience, to burst forth at certain moments in unforeseen shapes—with a Lessing for example.

---

beneath faith and mercy which, nevertheless, save it, without making us just from within; (b) in the sense that actual sins, which of themselves are excluded by faith (but which, through weakness, we commit in spite of faith) do not. however, make us lose the faith which saves us. Fantasies of an incurably nominalist theology which places opposites side by side.

[1] Cf. Karl Eschweiler, *die Philosophie der Spanischer Spätscholastik auf den Deutschen Universitäten des siebzehnten Jahrhunderts* 1928. *Spanische Forschungen der Görresegsellschaft*, Bd. I.

13. On Luther and Augustinianism, see the communication of M. l'abbé Paquier, the learned translator of Denifle, to the Philosophical Society of St. Thomas Aquinas, meeting of 21st February, 1923 (*Revue de philosophie*, March-April, 1923). The author there sums up the controversies raised by Müller, and pronounces his conclusions "hasty," and his affirmations "often guess-work." Yet we must not forget that in the Middle Ages, and even at the end of the Middle Ages, an Augustinianism flourished which was not unknown to Luther and must have influenced his theory of justification. "Luther," writes M. Paquier, "was far from being without an idea of the opposition between the two great schools, Augustinian and Thomist. In 1518 he wrote against Sylvester Priérias, Master of the Sacred Palace: 'For nearly *three hundred years* the Church has suffered from that unhealthy passion, that veritable lust which drives you to corrupt doctrine; an unparalleled injury, due to the scholastic doctors.' Two months after, he became definite and gave names: 'St. Thomas, St. Bonaventure, Alexander of Hales are certainly remarkable men; yet it is only right to prefer truth to them, and then the authority of the Pope and the Church. . . . *For more than three hundred years* the Universities, and so many remarkable men who have lived in them, have done nothing but toil over Aristotle, spreading his errors even more than the truth he may have taught.'" (Weim., I, 611, 21-28. cf. Enders II, 103-121.)

From this point of view, Lutheranism appears as a catastrophic incident in the old war waged against Thomism by the rash zeal of self-styled disciples of St. Augustine. None the less, if Luther found in Augustinian theologians a dangerous terminology and the theory, more or less stressed, for the formal identity of concupiscence and original sin, yet the drama of his religious experience and the "divine illumination" of the event in the Tower were needed for the internal logic of that theory to break out into heresy.

Let us recall that according to St. Thomas, the interpreter of the most authentic thought of St. Augustine and the echo of the whole Catholic tradition, concupiscence is only the *material* element of original sin; its persistence in us in no wise prevents original sin from being effaced by baptism, and sanctifying grace from residing intrinsically in our soul. (*Summa Theol.*, I-II, 82, 3.)

14. He who (duly enlightened) refuses his adherence to the revealed truths proposed by the *magisterium* of the Church, even on a single point, loses theological faith by that act. (Cf. St. Thomas: *Summa Theol.*, II-II, 5, 3.)

15. "My dear brother," Luther writes now, "you want to have the feeling of your justice, that is, to experience justice as you experience sin; that cannot be." (*In Galat.* [1535.] Weim., XL, P. II, 24, 27-29). "You must not listen to this feeling, but say: although I seem to be plunged in sin to the ears and to stifle in it, although my heart tells me that God has turned away from me and is angered against me, yet there is at bottom nothing true in all that, it is only a pure lie. . . So then, you are not bound to *feel* that you have justice, but to *believe* that you have it; if you do not believe that you are just, you commit a horrible blasphemy against Christ!" (Ibid, 31-32). He writes besides, (but the difference is only in expression, for he is speaking always of the security produced by faith-trust), "Christianity is nothing but a continual exercise in *feeling* that you have no sin, but that your sins are cast on Christ." (Opp. exeg. lat., XXIII, [142 1532-1534], Weim., XXV, 331, 7-16.) As early as 1518 he wrote, "It is a duty for us to believe that we are pleasing to God." (Weim., II, 46.)

As for himself, this exercise of faith-trust did not succeed in delivering him from sadness and anxiety. He had to fly to other means in temptations to despair. (*See* notes 21 and 35.)

16. Is it necessary to recall the fact that a "vital" act is an act which comes from our own proper and immanent activity whereby we move ourselves? Luther

denied that man could, under the action of grace, either prepare himself for justification or himself actively produce a really good work.

17. See the nine portraits in Denifle-Paquier and t. IV, p. 237 seq. We have taken four sufficiently characteristic ones from the series. Cf. equally Hans Preuss, *Luther-bildnisse :* Leipzig, 1912.

There is evidently a danger of subjective interpretation in constructing the inner state of a man from a series of portraits. That is why Denifle (or rather P. Weiss, conforming to his injunctions) has very wisely suppressed the *chapter* which he had devoted to *Luther from his portraits*. But the portraits themselves remain in the second edition, and rightly so. For there is no reason why we should not put before the reader iconographic documents, the significance of which each will appreciate, according to his taste and perspicacity.

We remarked, it is true, that the last of the portraits is "astoundingly bestial." This statement appears to us obvious,[1] though we quite understand that the admirers of Luther should think differently and we do not attempt to impose our opinion upon them. At any rate they cannot contest the engravings of the *Image de la Papauté*[2] which the Reformer gave to Matthias Wanckel as his *will* and which attests only too well the turn his imagination took in his last years.

18. We know what Luther's polemic was in regard to falsifications, calumnies, buffooneries, and obscenities (cf. Denifle's table, IV, 300, and the pamphlets about the Donkey-Pope, the Calf-Monk *The Image of the Papacy*, etc.). Falsehood never stopped him. "A necessary lie," he himself said of the bigamy of Philip of Hesse, "a useful lie, a helpful lie, none of these lies goes against God. . . .

[1] We have only reproduced four, among which do not appear two of the most significant—Nos. VI and VIII in the Denifle series.
[2] Cf. Denifle-Paquier, IV, 120; 265–277.

What harm would there be in telling a good big[1] lie for a greater good and for the sake of the Christian Church?" (Lenz: *Briefwechsel Landgraf Philipps von Hessen mit Bucer* I, 373-376.) On Luther and lying, cf. Denifle-Paquier, I, 218-224, Grisar, III, 1016-1019. It was not without justification that Duke George of Saxony called Luther "the most deliberate liar he had ever known." "We are bound to say and write of him that this apostate monk lies to our face like a damned scoundrel, dishonest and perjured." (19th December, 1528, in connexion with the Pack affair.) I recall here the methods by which the evangelical Reformation was imposed on the people in Saxony and the Scandinavian countries. The people, despite grave moral laxity, were relatively less corrupt than their temporal and spiritual heads, and besides, the goods stolen from the Church were not for them. They wanted to stay faithful to their religion; a brutal change would have provoked rebellions. What was to be done? Novelties in doctrine and cult were graded by a series of skilfully calculated measures so that they should be imperceptible; the people were separated from the communion of the Church without noticing it. Luther wrote in 1545, "Because our doctrine was then (shortly after his apostasy) new, and scandalized the masses all over the world, I had to go forward cautiously and leave aside many points because of the weak, which afterwards I did no longer." For example, as Melanchthon said, "people were so attached to the Mass that apparently nothing could tear it from men's hearts." (*Corp. Reform.*, I, 842.) Luther had therefore retained the Mass in Saxony in the official formularies of 1527 and 1528. The elevation of the Host and Chalice was kept. But Luther had suppressed the Canon without warning the public. "The priest," he said, "can very well manage so that the man of the people is still unaware of the change that has taken place,

---

[1] Instead of *Starke*, Walther wishes to read *Stracke Lüge*. (Für Luther weider Rom., 1906, p. 421). One would then translate "What harm would there be if . . . one lied roundly?" The root of the question is in no way changed by this variant.

and can assist at Mass without finding anything to scandalize him." In his tract on *the Celebration of the Mass in German* he said again, "The priests know the reasons which make it their duty to suppress the Canon," (Luther denied the *sacrifice* of the Mass); "as to laymen, it is useless to talk to them about it." In the same way Gustavus Vasa proclaimed to his people: "We want no other religion than that which our ancestors followed," and at the same time introduced heresy into his States.

On Luther's intemperance, cf. Denifle, I, 180-184. Luther, according to Melanchthon's testimony, could go four whole days without eating or drinking. "Often also he went several days without eating anything but a little bread and a herring." (Kuhn, I, 54.) But he knew how to make up for it. "I gorge like a Czech and I soak like a German," he wrote to Catherine Bora[1] (2nd

---

[1] M. Karl Holl reproaches us for having followed Janssen in quoting this letter to Catherine Bora (see moreover his answer to the criticisms of Köstlin in *Ein Zweites Wort an meine Kritiker*, 1883). No doubt this passage should be read in the spirit of heavy banter which Luther habitually used in his familiar conversation. It keeps however its peculiar flavour, particularly if one compares it with other quotations; for instance "Ego otiosus et crapulosus sedeo tota die" (1521 frau Wartbourg, Enders, III, 154); cf. also the famous letter to Weller (1530, Enders, VIII, 160, 72): "Why, do you suppose, do I drink too much wine, talk too much and like good meals too much? It is when the devil prepares to torment me and mock me and that I wish to take the lead." "Eat then," he says again to those who are troubled with bad thoughts, "drink, give yourself up to it with a light heart. When the body is tempted one must give it plenty to eat and to drink. It is the lecherous who must fast." (Mathesius, in Lösche, *Anal. Lutherana et Melanchthoniana* Gotha, 1892, No. 372, cited by Denifle-Paquier I, 182.) Denifle also quotes the testimony of the physician who examined Luther's body after death: "Owing to excess in eating and drinking his body was filled with decayed substances. Luther had, in fact, a copious board, and an over-abundance of sweet and foreign wines. It is said that every day at midday and in the evening he drank a pint of sweet and foreign wines." (Cf. Paulus, *Luthers Lebensende und der Eislebener Apothe ker Johann Landau*, Mainz, 1896.) We do not consider it a crime that Luther should have been a big eater and drinker; at least we may be allowed to remark that from this point of view the Gospel freed the former religious. Let us add that this note has no other object than to defend, against a criticism which is to our mind a little too arrogant, a quotation which we made *en passant*.

July, 1540, Burckhard: *Martin Luthers Briefwechsel* [1866], p. 357).

19. *Wider den falsch genannten geistlichen Stand*, 1522; Erl., 28, 199-200. In recalling these facts we are not following a frivolous desire for facile polemic nor the wish to make Lutheranism odious by the use of historical details chosen in a spirit of disparagement. Such kinds of argumentation are not to our taste. It is the common misfortune of the human race. Its burden of scandals makes them, quite justly, of little use. Also it is clear that one cannot impute the things in question to all those who followed Luther in the reform. Nevertheless they exist, and even if one guards against generalization they remain symptomatic of a period. Few sights are so shameful as the frenzy of sensuality which seized many of the seculars and regulars of both sexes liberated by Luther; gangrenous limbs only waiting occasion to fall from the body of the Church. To tell the truth, the decadence of the clergy was such that the situation could not last; either practice would have to rise to the level of theory by a triumph of holiness, or theory would have to fall to the level of practice by a triumph of concupiscence—which was the work of the Lutheran Reformation. What a deception! What a tragic mistake! Luther's aim was to save and renew *morality*. But going towards renouncement of "impossible" struggles, he sought the means of his reform in a polemic against the law and works instead of seeking it in Christian heroism and the victories of love.[1] The result, entirely contrary to his design, was inevitable. (He himself was to experience it in his own interior life, albeit remaining above the debaucheries which he deplored and bewailing excesses and scandals which he saw constantly going on around him.) One knows that priests and regulars many

---

[1] In truth he introduced in that way a new conception of morality itself, which is no longer defined as in *relation* to rule and as the conformity of heart to eternal laws, but becomes a sort of interior absolute, an absolute state of the heart (a feeling of liberty) given independently of the rule.

times exerted themselves, often in veritable gangs, to tear nuns from their cloisters and make them their "wives." Once the flight from the convent was accomplished, they came to unheard-of things; they held a sort of trade in profaned nuns; they veritably put them up for sale. "Nine of them have reached us," wrote one apostate priest to another, "they are beautiful, pleasing, and all of noble birth; none has reached her fiftieth year. For you, dear brother, I have kept the eldest to be your lawful wife, but if you want a younger one, you shall have your choice among the most beautiful." (Denifle, I, 27 28). It should be said that in this order of things, Luther did not so much create evil as set it free. And even that is a sufficiently heavy responsibility.

After a rape of nuns which took place on the night of *Holy Saturday*, 1523, Luther calls the citizen Koppe, who organized the exploit, a "blessed robber," and writes to him, "Like Christ, you have drawn these poor souls from the prison of human tyranny. You have done it at a time providentially indicated, at that moment of Easter when Christ destroyed the prison of His own." (*Ibid.*, 40; Weim., IX, 394–395.) He himself was surrounded by nuns thus restored to nature.[1] His Catherine Bora was one of them. It is curious to note that a base contempt for womanhood is the normal price of this war against Christian virginity. "The work and word of God tell us clearly that women must be used for marriage or prostitution." (Weim., XII, 94, 20-22 [1523].) "If women get tired and die of bearing, there is no harm in that; let them die, so long as they bear; they are made for that." (Erl., 20, 84; Weim., X, p. II, 301, 13, Sermon on Marriage, 1522.) And I quote only what can be transcribed.

Receive not the grace of God in vain, he cries to clerics when he invites them to break their vow of chastity. "There is only a short moment of shame to pass, then will come

---

[1] Nulla Phyllis nonnis est nostris mammosior, wrote the Lutheran Eoban Hesse. (Denifle, I, 189. *Helii Eobani Hessi et amicorum ipsius epp. famil. libri. XII*, Marpurgi, 1543, p. 87.)

the good years full of honour. May Christ give you His grace that, by His Spirit, these words may become life and power in your heart." (De Wette, II, 640.) He pours pity, itself morbid, on the poor young men and girls tormented by the fire of the senses (Enders, III, 207, August, 1521) and uses his evangelical zeal to deliver their *libido*, still declaring that "nothing can cure *libido*, not even marriage—*libido nullo remedio potest curari, nequidem conjugio,*—for the most married people live in adultery." (Opp. exeg. lat., I, 212, 26-27, 29-30 [1536.] Weim., XLII, 8-10.) In fact one can remark a certain relationship between the Lutheran *libido* and the Freudian *libido*. (Cf. Weim., XVI, 510-512, 5th November 1525.)

"Little by little," writes Denifle, "Luther thought, spoke and wrote, under the influence of a lustful delectation; thence came those writings (against chastity) the like of which could only be found—and even then but rarely—in the most depraved authors." (I, 172.) The sacrilegious mixture of immodesty and evangelicism of which he seems to have been the inventor is, from this point of view, characteristic. (Cf. Letter of 22nd July, 1525, Enders, V, 222; of the 6th December, 1825, Enders, V, 279.)

However unpleasant their subject may be, these historical indications give us an idea of Luther's moral state after his fall—a moral state which was its *result* much more than its *cause*. Such memories are, we believe, extremely disagreeable to the Lutherans of to-day, who are much more akin to the strictest puritanism than to the extremes and vagaries of Luther. One had, however, to recall them before plumbing their significance. There again the principle is spiritual. It is really the mystical fall which we indicate at the beginning of this chapter which is at the origin of Luther's polemic against celibacy: but now the strongly sensual religiosity has clearly slid on to the natural plane. It is always the interior liberty, the evangelic deliverance which he seeks; but now he puts as a condition the accomplishment of carnal desire, which the soul, to his mind, could not always constrain without enclosing itself in insurmountable torments of conscience and without renouncing spiritual peace for ever. Thus he always remains as *sincere* in his religious aspirations even when the inevitable law of the Destiny which he has chosen overtakes him. That is why he is such a terrible mixture of cynicism and candour, of prayer and lewdness. He has not understood that the sacrifices voluntarily imposed upon nature do not constrain, but deliver, when they are accomplished through love; neither has he understood that in the things of the spirit purity alone is fruitful, and inasmuch as it is precisely the condition of that liberty and of that peace which, according to St. Paul, is the privilege of the spiritual man. His hatred of *virginity* was essentially metaphysical and theological; that is what made it so pernicious.

It is not astonishing that the first effect of the preaching of the pure Gospel was, despite the complaints and objurgations of the wretched reformer, the worst overflow of animalism. As Heinrich Heine said, German history at that time is almost entirely composed of sensual disturbances. "The masses," declared Luther, "behave so scandalously towards the Gospel that the more one preaches the worse they become." (Erl., 17, 235-236 [1544].) "With this doctrine, the more we go forward, the worse the world becomes; it is the doing and work of that accursed devil. It is clear enough how much more greedy, cruel, immodest, shameless, wicked, the people now is than it was under Popery." (Erl., 1, 14 [1533].) "Adultery, fornication, and incest know no bounds," wrote Waldner. The worst was the corruption of youth. "Boys have no sooner left the cradle," wrote John Brenz in 1532, in a work prefaced by Luther, "than they at once want to have wives; and little girls who have a good time to wait before they are marriageable, spend their time dreaming of men." (Denifle, II, 111-115.) Freud's infantile psychology might have found verification in these little Lutherans born in an atmosphere tainted with lust, as perhaps it is verified in certain specially *prepared* environments in the twentieth century.

20. "The Papists put in heaven people who could only string works together; there is not one, among so many legends of saints, which shows us a true saint, a man possessing the true Christian sanctity, sanctity by faith. All their sanctity consists in having prayed much, fasted much, worked much, in their having mortified themselves, had a bad bed and clothing which was too coarse. Dogs and pigs, too, can almost practise this kind of sanctity daily." (Erl., 63, 304 [1531].)

21. Enders VIII, 160-161 (1530). We do not overlook the fact that this letter to Jerome Weber is a thorn in the side of Luther's apologists. This reason is not, however, sufficient to prevent us quoting it. Would any efforts of exegesis ever bring one, according to the words of Fr. Denifle (Denifle-Paquier II, 131²) "not to see that Luther tries to expel one devil with another"? The original quality of his *moralism*, his central preoccupation of calming consciences and producing at any cost in souls *a moral state* appears here in the most remarkable manner. Let us give the end of the passage already quoted: "Oh! if I could only find a good sin to make a fool of the devil, to make him understand fully that I do not recognize any sin, and that my conscience does not reproach me with any. We who are thus attacked and tormented by the devil absolutely must put the whole Decalogue from our eyes and from our spirit."

22. "Since there is no more to be hoped for from the Papists, since all fair dealing with them is useless," cries Luther (in his pamphlet *Wider den Meuchler zu Dresden* [1531]), "henceforth, till I am in my tomb I will curse and inveigh against those wretches, they'll not hear another good word from me. I wish to strike them, until they give way under my thunder and my lightning."

"Inasmuch as I cannot pray, I must curse. Instead of saying: 'Hallowed be Thy name,' I will say: 'Cursed, damned, abhorred be the name of the Papists!' Instead of saying: 'Thy Kingdom come,' I will say: 'Cursed, damned,

G

exterminated be the Papacy with all the kingdoms of the earth which are against Thy rule.' Instead of saying: 'Thy will be done,' I will say: 'Cursed, damned, abhorred and annihilated be all the plots of the Papists and all those who stand against Thy will and Thy counsel.' In truth that is how I pray every day without ceasing with my lips and with my heart, and with me, all who believe in Christ . . ." (Erl. 25, 108). [To Karl Holl (Rev. de théol. and phil., art. cit.) "all that Luther says is quite intelligible and inoffensive," because considering the Pope an Anti-Christ he could not say the Our Father without wishing at the same time, the ruin of the Papacy. Pleasant and gentle exegesis! The question is whether, hating the Pope and Catholics with the same hatred that one has for the devil (for that is what it really comes to) is "quite inoffensive." One knows Luther's ferocious hate of the Pope, Papists and the clergy: "May it please God to send down upon them the rain of fire and sulphur which consumed Sodom and Gomorrah, and to cast them into the sea that their very memories may be effaced";[1] good Christians ought to "wash their hands in the blood of Papists."[2] "The Pope, Cardinals and the whole crowd of idolatrous Papists ought to be hung, the tongues of the blasphemers pulled out by the roots and nailed to the gallows in the way that they affix their seals to Bulls";[3] he wishes the Papacy and all its followers in the infernal regions;[4] to him it is a sign that one loves God if one hates the Pope.[5] In 1537 leaving Schmalkalde, and believing himself to be on the point of death, he gave those surrounding him this supreme blessing, "Impleat vos Dominus benedictione sua et odio papae."[6] To introduce this hate and these maledictions into prayer

---

[1] Weim., VIII, 624 (1521).
[2] Weim., VI, 347 (1520).
[3] Erl., XXVI, 155 (1545).
[4] Erl., XXV, 88 (1531).
[5] *In Galat.*, Weim., XL, p. i. 576, 25.
[6] Preface of Veit Dietrich, *in opp. exeg. lat. XXV*, 135 (Denifle-Paquier, III, 455).

itself, to insert it in each request of Sunday prayers, all this we agree is "comprehensible" on the part of the Reformer. We doubt whether it is "quite inoffensive."]

One can see in Denifle-Paquier, IV, 18 seq., the way in which Luther drove away the devil when he tempted him by thoughts of anguish and sadness, showing him his sins. In this connection Denifle quotes *Martini Lutheri Colloquia*, ed. Bindseil (1863-1866) II, 299: "Hae pessimae cogitatones me plus vexaverunt, quam omnes mei infiniti labores. Quoties meam uxorem complexus sum, nudam contrectavi, ut tantum Sathanae cogitationes illo pruritu pellerem." It was labour lost: "Nolebat cedere." These agonizing melancholies really only tortured Luther more and more, in spite of faith-trust fortified by such remedies. "Sadness of heart is not pleasing to God; but although I know that I fall into that feeling a hundred times a day. However, I resist the devil." (Erl., 60, 129.) Cf. The *Tagebuch* of Cardatus born 1652. (Weim., *Tischreden* III, 257, 30-32) and that of Lauterbach, p. 50 (ibid., 625, 20-35; 626, 1-16.)

23. The latest French historian of Luther, M. Lucien Febvre,[1] rightly looks upon as demolished—thanks, however, to Denifle who is quickly "demolished" in his turn—the old version of Luther's life put forward for so long in the official Protestant hagiography. (In addition he seems not to know, among other recently published German works, the efforts of Karl Holl to renew the official version according to the antiquated formula of a pious liberalism.)

Troubling himself little with theology and reducing excessively, even with regard to a Luther, the importance of doctrinal questions, animated on the other hand by a strong aversion not only for the Catholic Church but also for Christianity in general, M. Lucien Febvre attenuates and excuses what he can and, for the rest, conceding cleverly what must be conceded, he opposes to the apology on pharisaical lines, an apology on cynical lines better

[1] Lucien Febvre, *Un destin: Martin Luther*, Paris, Rieder. 1928.

adapted to our time. Which is to say that he uses a scale of values quite different from ours. Apart, however, from his judgements of values and simply from the point of view of the psychological reconstruction there is, on quite a number of points, agreement between the portrait which he shows of Luther and the one we give here, an agreement which we do not find it unpleasant to note.

24. Cf. St. Thomas, *Summa Theol.*, I-II, 112, 5; De Verit., X, 10; in II Cor., 13, lect. 2. St. Bonaventure, 1 Sent. dist. 17, pars 1, q. 3; 3 Sent., dist. 26, ma. 1, q. 5: "Haberi potest certitudo per probabilem conjecturam et per quamdam confidentiam, quae consurgit ex conscientia bona." Alexander of Hales (3 p., q. 71, m. 3, a. 1): "Nec dimisit nos Deus penitus in gratiae ignorantia, quia dedit nobis ut cognosceremus ipsam secundum affectivam cognitionem in experientia et sensu divinae dulcedinis, quae est ex gratia." And a. 2: "Concedendum quod per scientiam experimentalem possumus scire nos habere gratiam."

25. "For him, then, there could only be question of soteriology, and that in this sense, that *man remained its central point*. To-day, Protestant theologians take pleasure in the thought that Christ is the centre of Luther's "system." Nothing is more untrue, and nothing more in contradiction to the conclusions of a psychological inquiry into the process of his evolution. *Although it speaks often of Christ, the centre of Luther's theology is not Christ, but man.*" (Denifle-Paquier, III, 249-250. Italicised in the text.)

26. We say that *in actual fact* it is an inevitable result of Luther's theology. That does not prevent the same theology from running, simultaneously and *in theory*, to the opposite extreme. (It is not uncommon in Luther as in Descartes to find an extreme error counterbalancing another error diametrically opposed to it.) So Luther tells us

that salvation and faith are so much the work of God
and of Christ that they alone are the agents without any
active co-operation on our part.[1]

"Homo antequam renovetur in novam creaturam
regni spiritus, nihil facit, nihil conatur, quo paratur ad
eam renovationem et regnum; deinde renovatus, nihil
facit, nihil conatur, quo perseveret in eo regno, sed
utrumque facit solus spiritus in nobis, nos sine nobis
recreans et conservans recreatos . . . sed non operatur sine
nobis ut quos in hoc ipsum recreavit et conservat, ut
operaretur in nobis et nos ei cooperaremur." An entirely
passive and material co-operation (since we remain
radically bad) which consists only in submitting to
Divine action, in order that it may draw from us the works
of the new man (but without our own action intervening
or our liberty being exercised). It is in this *completely
passive* sense that we become "new creatures" and that
God acts in us and through us. "Sic per nos praedicat,
miseretur pauperibus, consolatur afflictos. Verum quid
hinc libero arbitrio tribuitur? Imo quid ei relinquitur
nisi nihil? Et vere nihil." (*De servo arbitrio*, Weim.,
XVIII, 754.) From this point of view Denifle is right
in maintaining that Luther's theory of faith is full of contradictions and is even made impossible (for according
to St. Augustine belief depends upon our free activity:
"Credere vel non credere in libero arbitrio est voluntatis
humanae," *de Praed.* Sanct V. 10) and that it only remains
to say that it is not we who believe, but God Himself Who
believes in us.

"Fides opus est omnium operum excellentissimum et
arduissimum," writes Luther (*De captiv. Babyl.*, 1520;
Weim., VI, 530) " . . . Est opus Dei, non hominis, sicut

---

[1] "He alone commands and alone fulfils." (Von der Freiheit eines
Christenmenschen, Weim, VII, 24.) "Nostrum agere est pati operantem
in nobis Deum." (*In Galat.* 1535, Weim., XL, Pt. 610, 17.) "He who
wishes to uphold freewill in man and to maintain, howsoever restrict-
edly, that in the spiritual order it is capable of anything and can
give it support, that man denies Christ. I hold to that, and I know
that it is the very truth." (*Tischreden*, Weim., VI, 119, 10–13, No
6683.)

dicit Paulus; caetera nobiscum et per nos operatur, hoc unicum in nobis et sine nobis operatur."

The co-operation (*nobiscum et per nos*) which he mentions with regard to other works is already quite passive and material, as we have just seen, and now he excludes this same co-operation from the work of faith (*sine* nobis)! Denifle has carefully noted the way in which Luther warped the scholastic formulæ, of which he knew little concerning the infusion of supernatural virtues (Denifle-Paquier, III, 273-274). He might have added that Luther deforms and corrupts in the same way the scholastic theory concerning *gratia operans*.

M. Karl Holl (*Revue de théol. et de phil. art. cit.*) accuses Denifle and us of having suppressed the "Christ within us" of Luther's Christology. M. Karl Holl does not understand the question in point. Neither has he read the "in fact" which qualifies all our development.[1]

We never thought of denying (nor has Denifle so far as we know) the part played in theory, by the "Christ within us" in Lutheran theology. The question is, whether Christ acts in us *by* and *with our own proper activity* or *without it*. The moment we believe in *determinism*, and the essential and irremediable corruption of our nature: the moment we no longer understand that man, made by grace *consors divinae naturæ* acts of himself, freely and meritoriously, under the action of God and Christ, as a secondary cause, subordinated to the *first* cause—so that our good acts come entirely from ourselves as secondary causes, and altogether from God as principal cause, and that we are only the first cause in the order of evil—then we much either attribute salvation and good works to Jesus Christ alone, acting in us without our own active co-operation, or make everything depend upon the impulse of faith and confidence which comes from us alone, whereby we attain the merits of Christ.

Luther's theology will vary without ceasing between these two solutions; in theory it appears to be the first which will prevail, but as it is psychologically impossible

[1] Cf. p. 3.

to eliminate human activity, it is the second which will
de facto prevail.

When Luther's theology teaches that Christ fulfils the
law for us, it varies constantly between the idea that
works prescribed by divine law are done *by another* IN US
(without the co-operation of our own activity)—that is
why it is sufficient to have faith, good works necessarily
follow—and the idea that the works of the law have been
accomplished *by another* IN OUR PLACE—that is why it is
enough to have faith; and so, were we to sin a thousand
times a day, we should nevertheless be saved and accepted
by God. Here again, because psychologically faith alone
will not prevent us falling or make us produce good works
inevitably, it is the second idea which *actually* prevails
in practice. It is easy to go from a law which is fulfilled
in us by another to a law which we do not fulfil.

27. St. Thomas, *Summa Theol.*, I, 60, 5; II-II, 61, I; 64,
2, 5; 65, 1. As Cajetan (*in* I, 60, 5) remarks against
Scotus, it is not because it finds its proper good in the whole
but because, as a part, it is essentially related to the whole
and only exists for it, that the part, as such, prefers the
whole to itself and sacrifices if necessary its own good to
the common good, as the hand sacrifices itself if necessary
for the body. "Non ergo ratio inclinationis talis est
identitas, aut ut salvet seipsam in toto, sed ut salvet esse
totius secundum se, etiam cum non esse ipsius partis.
Sed ratio talis inclinationis est quam assignavit sanctus
Thomas quia scilicet et natura et substantia partis hoc
ipsum quod est, essentialiter, et primo propter totum
et totius esse est."

Let us add that man, if he is a *part* of the city,
regarded as an individual having need of his fellow
creatures in order to complete, here below, his specific
work (civilization)—in this sense St. Thomas teaches that
all his acts, inasmuch as they are susceptible of human,
exterior communication can be referred to the good of
the political community[1]—yet regarded formally as a

[1] "Et secundum hoc actus omnium virtutum ad justitiam pertinere,
secundum quod ordinat hominem ad bonum commune." (II–II, 58, 5.)

person destined for God, he is, on the contrary, possessed of the character of a whole and escapes the political order. *Homo non ordinatur ad communitatem politicum secundum se totum et secundum omnia sua* (*Summa Theol.* I-II, 21, 4 ad 3).

In his "*Leçons de Philosophie Sociale*" (t. 1, p. 14 seq.) it was Fr. Schwalm who drew attention to this point but he did not avoid certain obscurities and confusions. Let us note, in particular, that if man "*naturaliter est pars alicujus multitudinis per quam praestetur sibi auxilium ad bene vivendum.*" This means that *as a part* his good is subordinate to the good of the community like the imperfect to the perfect, and not that society is subordinated to the good of each individual. (Schwalm, p. 17.)

On the other hand in the following text (ibid., p. 23) "*Totus homo ordinatur ut ad finem ad totam communitatem cujus est pars*" (II-II, 65, 1), the words *totus homo* as is shown by the context, refer to the integrity of the corporal members (the question is "utrum in aliquo casu possit esse licitum mutilare aliquem membra sua") and not to that which integrates the human being: for from that point of view the express teaching of St. Thomas, as we have said above, is that "man is not subordinated to the political community as to his whole person, and as to all that belongs to him."

28. St. Thomas: *Summa Theol.*, I-II, 2, 8; Summa contra Gent., III, 48; in Polit. Arist. (lib. 3, c. 9), lect. 7. In ad 3 of q. 64, a. 2, IIa-IIae, St. Thomas explains that if the death penalty is legitimate, it is not only because the guilty man has become, by his crime a destroyer of the common good, but also because by choosing to fall from the order of reason, he has entered in some way into the slavery belonging to the beasts, which are only for the use of others. "Et ideo quamvis hominem in sua dignitate manentem occidere sit secundum se malum, tamen hominem peccatorem occidere potest esse bonum, sicut occidere bestiam: pejor enim est malus homo, quam bestia, et plus nocet, ut Phil. dicit in I. Politic. (cap. 2) et in 7 Ethic. (cap. 6)." And the punishment of death,

by giving the man opportunity to restore the order of reason in himself by an act of conversion to the Last End, does precisely allow him to recover his dignity as a human person.

29. *Sum. Theol.*, II-II, 26, 4. One must fully understand this doctrine. We do not say that the person itself, the subject responsible for its action and capable of virtue, is not a part of the city! This would be absurd, "quaelibet persona singularis comparatur ad totum communitatem sicut pars ad totum." II-II, 64, 2. And the acts of all the virtues are *to be referred* to the good of the city (ibid., 58, 5) which itself is a human and moral good.

We say that the single person (itself) can be considered either under the formal aspect of an individual part of the city or under the formal aspect of a person destined to God: in the first case its own good is to be referred to the good of the community, in the second case it is that common temporal good which is to be referred to its interests, spiritual and eternal.

This doctrine of individuality and of personality is at the very roots of Thomist metaphysics. The whole theory of "individuation" shows that for St. Thomas the individual as such is *a part*. (Even in the angel, where the principal of individuation is the specific essence itself, not the matter, it is because the essence—really distinct in respect of its existence and potency—is the ground of multiplicity, that it is also a ground of individuality.) On the other hand for St. Thomas, the idea of personality bespeaks as such independence of a *whole*. In the same way it alone, with the notion of object of knowledge, denotes a term which can, while making one with something else, not imply in any manner the rôle of a part; this is the reason why God who cannot "enter into composition" with anything at all nor be part of a whole, cannot be united by himself to a creature except either as an object intelligible in the beatific vision (*in ratione puri termini objectivi*) or as a person in the Incarnation (*in ratione puri termini personalis*). In the Holy Trinity the idea of personality reaches the plenitude of pure act. One has then a society divinely perfect, where three persons equal and consubstantial have for common good their own nature, and where each is as much as the three together, in other words, where the notion of individuation and part has entirely disappeared.[1]

30. On the metaphysical idea of servitude, cf. St. Thomas, *Sum. Theol.*, I, 96, 4. To take the word in its exact sense, that person is in servitude who finds himself under the government of another for the sake of the private utility of the latter (and not for the sake of the good of the subject himself or the common good). That is a penal state consequent upon the sin of Adam. If in its harder form this status, which, even when it does not amount to a violation of the natural law and the essential rights of the human person, is repugnant to the spirit of the New Testament, has been gradually abolished by the influence of Christianity, it will be noticed, nevertheless, that it still exists in less apparent forms, and that the modern idea of "proletariat," for example, conforms to the very strict meaning, defined by St. Thomas. It is to be presumed that in one form or another, which we may hope will be less and less cruel, it will subsist as long as the *results* of original sin.

31. "Bonum commune civitatis et bonum singulare unius personae non differunt secundum multum et paucum, sed secundum formalem differentiam. Alia est enim ratio Boni communis et Boni singularis, sicut alia ratio totius et partis. Et ideo Philosophus in 1. Politic dicit quod non bene dicunt qui dicunt civitatem et domum et alia hujusmodi differre solum multitudine et paucitate, et non specie." *Summa Theol.*, II-II, 58, 7, ad 2.

32. "Quia igitur vitae, qua in praesenti bene vivimus, finis est beatitudo coelestis, ad regis officium pertinet ea

[1] "Si autem accipiamus numerum prout est in rebus numeratis, sic in rebus quidem creatis, unus est pars duorum, et duo trium, ut unus homo duorum et duo trium; et sic non est in Deo quia tantus est pater, quanta tota est trinitas (*Sum. Theol.*, I, 30, 1, ad 4)."

ratione vitam multitudinis bonam procurare, secundum quod congruit ad coelestem beatitudinem consequendam, ut scilicet ea praecipiat, quae ad coelestem beatitudinem ducunt, et eorum contraria, secundum quod fuerit possibile, interdicat. Quae autem sit ad veram beatitudinem via, et quae sint impedimenta ejus, ex lege divina cognoscitur, cujus doctrina pertinet ad sacerdotum officium." St. Thomas, *De Regimine principum*, I, 15. Hence the *indirect power* of the Church over civil society. Cf. Garrigou-Lagrange, de Revelatione, II, 440 ff.

33. *Nostrae vitae tragedia*, Weim., I, 92. A word very true in itself, but in the doctrine of Luther it bears on a human nature rooted in evil, like a fallen angel which Christ saves as by a *coup*, by violence contrary to the nature of things, as one might save, to suppose the impossible, a sort of demon. So the tragedy of human life took the colour of angelical despair which was to become so astounding in the modern world.

The cry of a Christian, "Without you we can do nothing," a cry of enraptured joy, an *amen* where nature and grace kissed, becomes now a shriek of anguish.

34. Luther himself was certainly not a modern man, any more than he was a *Protestant*. But this does not prevent him from being at the origin of the modern world just as he is at the origin of Protestantism. And that is just what makes his case so interesting. A ruined Catholic, a spoilt Saint, it is in his false, insane, and altogether egocentric way of throwing himself on certain old truths,[1] too much forgotten by those around him, that one sees appearing in him the principal modern errors.

And is it not thus, according to St. Thomas, that the great primordial sins were produced? The sin of the angels and the sin of Adam: they wished for something

---

[1] E.g. confidence in Jesus Christ, contempt for oneself, the value of conscience as an immediate judge of our actions, and for fallen man the impossibility of attaining to a natural perfection without the grace of Christ, etc.

good in itself—resemblance to God—*in a wrong way*. Men
like Luther are violators of truth. We are quite prepared
to believe with M. Jean Baruzi[1] that Luther adheres
more closely to *Taulerian* mysticism—though at the same
time he degrades it—than is generally thought.

If by some inevitable fate Luther's revolt was to be the
far-off progenitor of liberation, private judgement, etc.,
originally it appeared under a totally different guise.
As has often been remarked, it was, like Jansenism, a
reactionary heresy with its eyes fixed on the past. Such
are the most tenacious heresies in religion, while in the
secular order it is, on the contrary, error in the name of
novelty that succeeds.

Against the semi-rationalism of Gabriel Biel and of
decadent scholasticism, Luther rears an exaggerated religious
sentiment, fed on an Augustinianism vitiated and very soon
completely falsified.

It may be seen how certain Protestant critics (M. René
Gollouir, M. Louis Dallière) have been able to misunder-
stand our position: because we consider Luther to be the
father of modern individualism, they have thought that
we made him an individualist, in the modern sense of the
word. Such was never our idea. That the idea of
individualistic religion would have horrified Luther, that
he always loved the "idea of the Church," and even at
the moment of his breaking with her, pretended to be
serving the Church against the Pope, of this we are as
much convinced as M. Dallière.[2] But in freeing the
Christian communities from the Roman tyranny, and
from the spiritual authority of the vicar of Christ, he was
really freeing them from the unity of the Body of Christ,
only to imprison them, in spite of himself, in the temporal
body of the political and national community, and to
subject them finally to the authority of the Princes whom
he hated. National individualism (cujus regio ejus religio)

---

[1] Cf. Jean Baruzi—*Luther, interprète de St. Paul* (Revue de Théo. et
de Philos., janvier-mars, 1928).
[2] Louis Dallière *La réalite de l'église, étude théologique et religieuse* (Mont-
pellier, juillet, 1927, pp. 422–427).

was soon to appear as the inevitable result of the conquest of Christian liberty. In addition the spiritual principle of Luther's Reform, by a fatal logic, incomparably stronger than Luther himself, was bound to bear its fruits.

35. "From 1530, when his doctrine had come fully into practice, there was everywhere an increase of melancholy, of gloomy sadness, of agonies of despair, of doubt of the divine grace, and of suicides. . . . Enough *books of consolation* cannot be written against the fear of death and the wrath of God, against sadness and melancholy, against doubt about the grace of God and eternal happiness. Until then, nothing like it had been seen.

"In the spectacle which the preachers afford us here there is a bitter irony; they cannot boast enough about the consolation which the new 'Gospel' brings, as opposed to the agony produced by Catholic doctrine, and yet they are compelled to draw attention publicly to the increase of sadness and suicide. . . . 'Never was need of consolation so keenly felt as in our days.' (Magdeburgius: *A fine remedy to soothe the pains and sorrows of suffering Christians,* Lübeck, 1555.) Indeed, "more than ever we hear alas, daily, that either in full health or in the hour of their agony people fall into despair, lose their reason, and, some at least, go so far as to kill themselves." (Baumgärtner.) . . . Neither Luther himself, nor his panegyrist Mathesius, nor Leonard Beyer, he, too, formerly an Augustinian and then pastor at Guben, nor others beside, could escape the temptation to have done with life, to such a degree that when they were in that state it was dangerous for them to have a knife at hand. . . . George Besler, one of the first propagators of Lutheranism at Nuremberg, fell into such deep melancholy that in 1536 he left his wife in the middle of the night and plunged a hunting-spear full in his breast. . . . In the agonies of death and in temptations Luther did not succeed in living his faith. Nor was it otherwise with his believers, with those among his people who were "pious." We know it already of his friend Jerome Weller; others of his friends were in the same case

George Spalatin, Justus Jonas, Mathesius, Nicolas Hausmann, George Rorarius; and other leaders of the Reformation: Flaccius Illyricus, William and Balthasar Bidembach, Joachim Mörlin, Chemnitz, Isinder of Königsberg, Andrew Gundelwein, and a host of others who fell, more or less, especially in their last years, into overwhelming agonies, into an incurable sadness, and even into madness, without the consolations of Luther and others being any use to them." Denifle, IV, 23-27. Cf. Döllinger: *Die Reformation*, II, 688 ff.

36. Erl., 16, 142 to 148 (1546). Cf. Denifle-Paquier. III, 277-278. If the practical result aimed at by Luther, above all else, be to exhort his hearers to act according to faith and not according to human reason only, this does not take anything away from the diseased falsity and absurdity of the formulæ to which he has recourse.

37. Luther often employs statements (especially in the period of the *Commentary on the Epistle to the Romans*) which he derived from traditional Catholic teaching. But the more his theology crystallised in opposition to Catholic Theology, the more impossible it became for him to make room, I do not say for the word, but for the right idea of charity. It is clear that charity, which is not any love of God, but a *friendship* between God and man founded upon supernatural participation in the divine nature, and an efficacious friendship, which drives that corruption of mortal sin from the soul and makes us produce works that are intrinsically good, is necessarily excluded from a system in which man is in himself irremediably bad. Luther never understood the scholastic doctrine of *fides formata caritate*. His polemics on this subject are well known. They are more important than his polemics against good works, for they are the principle of these, just as charity is the principle of good works Luther so completely misunderstands the truth that charity is infused participation in the very life of God and Christ, which Christ's blood has bought for us: he is so blinded

on this point, that in his opinion one rejects Christ and
makes Him unnecessary, if one makes salvation depend
upon charity.[1] For then, according to him, we should
have been justified, not in Christ but in ourselves. Christ
would be innocent of our sins and these would, in reality,
fall back upon us. "Somniant enim fidem quamdam
formatam caritate; per hanc contendunt tolli peccata et
justificari homines, quod plane est Christum exuere et
evolvere peccatis eumque facere innocentem, et nos ipsos
gravare et ebruere peccatis propriis, et ea intueri non in
Christo, sed in nobis, quod vere est tollere et otiosum
reddere Christum."[2] He exhorts his disciples to be piously
obdurate against the Papists on this point (*hic volumus et
debemus esse rebelles et pertinaces*) or they would lose faith
in Christ.[3] And, on the pretext that charity is the object
of a precept and of the precept *par excellence*, he goes so
far as to identify charity with one of those *works of the law*
which by themselves are not enough to justify man.[4]
"Ibi (sc. in justificatione) certe nullum est opus legis,
nulla dilectio sed longe alia justitia et novus quidam mundus
extra et supra legem."[5]

And Luther can even keep the name of charity, saying
that although serving for nothing in justification, yet, as

---

[1] According to Catholic teaching good works are not the cause of
our justification, they are rather the products and manifestation of it.
(Cf. St. Thomas *in Galat.*, III, 10 lect. 4). It is the sanctifying grace
of infused charity which makes man just in the eyes of God. Faith is
the root and foundation of all our justice because it is the root and
foundation of charity. By it we are saved and justified when it is perfected, and in so far as it is perfected, in an efficacious love of God
above all things (*fides caritate formata*). And if good works, which come
from our free, human activity, *deified* by the grace of Christ and supernatural gifts, are necessary for our salvation, it is because it is impossible
to love God efficaciously above all things without acting in consequence,
or to choose a created good for final end, without losing charity.

[2] *In Galat.* (1535), Weim., XL, P. I, 436, 27-31. Cf. *Opp.* exeg.,
lat., III, 302 (1538): "Si fides formatur a caritate, *igitur opera praecipuum
illud sunt, quod respicit Deus; Si autum opera, ergo nos ipsi.*" (Weim.,
XLII, 565, 5-8).

[3] Ibid., Weim., XL, P. I, 167, 20-21.

[4] *In Galat.* (1525), Weim., XL, P. I, 225, 226, 239-241; 605-606.

[5] Ibid., 229, 30-32.

in other virtues, it accompanies faith. The reality of
charity can no more exist for him than can any activity
which, proceeding vitally from man and his faculties,
proceeds at the same time from God, and would be
intrinsically good, holy and meritorious. Doubtless he
does not suppress all love of God, but then it is no longer
a question of *Charity*, it is a question of a thankfulness
to God following upon salvation through faith alone,
which is fundamentally incapable of making us adhere
to God as to our friend, and of making us, according to
the truth of apostolic teaching, "one spirit" with Him.
*Christus autem non est lex, ergo nec exactor legis nec
operum, sed est Agnus Dei, qui tollit peccata mundi.
Hoc sola fides apprehendit non caritas, quae quidem fidem sequi
debet,* SED UT GRATITUDO QUAEDAM (*In Galat.*, 1535, Weim.,
XL, P. I, 241, 18–21).

Finally—and logically—Faith as Harnack remarked in
his *Das Wesen des Christentums*, (4th ed., p. 169–170) *is
the only thing which God wants from us.* "You have no other
duty to God than to believe in Him and to confess Him"
(Weim., XII, 131 [1523].) *Charity is for your neighbour.*
"Understood according to the sophists, the infused virtues
of hope and charity are to be rejected: the object of
charity is your neighbour, of faith is God." (*Disputationen,* ed. Drews, p. 732, n. 7, 16 and 17.) "Faith is
concerned only with God and remains in the heart; charity
is occupied with our neighbour, and acts externally."
(Ibid., p. 178.) "The Christian," he wrote as early as
1520, "does not live within himself but in Christ, and in
his neighbour, otherwise he is not a Christian: in Christ
through faith, in his neighbour through charity. Faith
lifts him above himself towards God, *charity brings him
down again towards his neighbour.*" (*De Libertate Christiana,*
Weim., VII. 69, cf., *in Galat.*, 1535. Weim., XL., P. II,
37–38.) Nothing is more disastrous than this abasement
of charity turned from its first object. The progress of this
mistake may be seen through the whole of modern times.

It matters little whether the Reformer clearly realized
it or not, or that he should have contradicted himself

frequently on the point; one must, in these conditions, say with Denifle that the worship of God will become more and more the worship of man, God asking nothing of us, neither works nor gifts, and man having no value but in relation to his neighbour. (Denifle-Paquier, III, 413.) On this point, as Fr. Weiss has remarked, the Lutheran conception of religion already introduces "something like the religion according to Kant."

If one wished (at this point) to set in relief the profound significance of Lutheranism one would have to say, we think, that Luther no more understood the rôle of charity as the ultimate *form* of justification and of the moral life than he understood in evil, the rôle of the ultimate constituting *form* of sin. Thenceforth we cannot understand the theory of a dead faith: for him it can only be the corpse of faith, a faith which does not exist: he cannot see that it is a real faith—living as to the supernatural adhesion of the intelligence to revealed truth—but dead as to the ordering, by the form (extrinsic) and the direction of charity, to its final end.

And equally, he is unable to see that in the just man sin can be dead as to its *ultimate formality* (intrinsic) *while continuing alive as to all the material of its dispositions and tendencies.*

"The sin which lives in me"—ἡ ἐνοικοῦσα ἐν ἐμοι ἁμαρτία, says St. Paul; and it is one of the texts which struck Luther most forcibly.

But St. Paul also says that he is dead to sin and sin dead to him. Both are true: all sin—the very living tendencies—can live in a just soul, except the form of sin. And concupiscence is never completely absent. But the form of sin itself is not there; as to this form (through which the will of the soul is turned from its final end) sin is dead in the just. For Luther, on the contrary, who has quarrelled with formal and material causality (as with Aristotle their father) and who only knows barbarous psychological aspects and inaction, (Weim., IV, 664, I, 486), the Christian who is justified is, at the same time and formally, just and sinful, *simul peccator et justus* (Ficker,

II, 108). Whence it follows that sin is no longer the opposite of grace, a consequence drawn by Rousseau while waiting for the modern *marriage of heaven and hell*. And this justice does not depend upon charity, a form of saving faith, it depends upon *fiducia*—wherein faith and hope seem to *mix* and where is a living faith without charity; charity (which he makes, as we saw above, a very impoverished concept), is but the sign and effect of faith.

38. Letter to Melanchthon, 1st August, 1521. Enders, III, 208. "Si gratiae praedicator es, gratiam non fictam, sed veram praedica; si vera gratia es, verum non fictum peccatum ferto. Deus non facit salvos ficte peccatores. Esto peccator et pecca fortiter, sed fortius fide et gaude in Christo, qui victor est peccati, mortis et mundi. Peccandum est, quandiu sic sumus; vita haec non est habitatio justitiae, sed expectamus, ait Petrus, coelos, novos, et terram novam, in quibus justitia habitat. Sufficit quod agnovimus per divitias gloriae Dei agnum, qui tollit peccatum mundi; ab hoc non avellet nos peccatum, etiam si millies, millies uno die fornicemur aut occidamus. Putas tam parvum esse pretium et redemptionem pro peccatis nostris factam in tanto et tali agno? Ora fortiter, es enim fortissimus peccator." Few passages show better than this celebrated text, the apologia for dead faith, the tragic corruption of the highest truths wrought by heresy. The intention of Luther is to restore confidence to the soul, overwhelmed by the feeling of its sin. And it is, of course, true that we must take refuge increasingly in our confidence in the sovereign merits of Christ our Redeemer, according as we realize more fully that we are sinners, i.e. that the *fomes peccati* or concupiscence, remains in us (which is not original sin itself but the permanent wound left by original sin) in addition, perhaps, to strong and formidable tendencies to sin. Equally it is true that even in mortal sin, even should we fall back a thousand times into sin, we must again hope in these infinite merits.

But what we hope then, is that through those merits
and by His efficacious help (formal motive of the virtue of
hope) God will give us sanctifying grace, will admit us
and maintain us in His friendship, which regenerates us
interiorly and drives out—no doubt not the kernel of
concupiscence (nor venial sin)—but certainly mortal sin,
as light drives out darkness: and which is incompatible
with that sin as light is incompatible with darkness.
Thus, indeed, mortal sin, which causes one to lose that
grace, is really for a Christian the worst catastrophe, the
evil *par excellence*, rather than which one must choose any
suffering and death in any form. As for Luther, he does
not care a straw whether this doctrine retains its proportions and its equilibrium. He is wholly possessed by
a sort of worldly pity, freed from the bounds of charity,
which is one of the elements of its tragic greatness: a pity
which is more *human* (that is, *too* human) than Christian
(which means *super*human): a pity which is simply compassion for the sinner originating less from brotherhood
with the Saviour and with the divine love, than from a
painful brotherhood in the old slough of misery of sin
itself.

So he allows himself to be carried away by this mania
for theological hyperbole, for diseased exaggeration, which
is his own special way of preserving truth: he asserts that
salvation can be gained by faith alone; he asserts the
compatibility of the state of sin in which we have remained
fixed by our nature since Adam, with a grace, a love and
a *confidence* powerless to make us internally and really just
and friends of God, which yet assure us forgiveness and
salvation. Thus the just have always one foot in sin and
one in grace. "Sic justus semper est in peccato pede sinistro
et vetere homine, et in gratia pede dextro, i.e. novo
homine." (Sermon of the 27 December, 1514—or according to Denifle, 1515.) Thus grace in all its verity and
reality (*gratia vera non ficta*) co-exists in the just man with
sin with all its verity and reality (*verum non fictum peccatum*)—
not only the tendencies to sin, but sin itself, formal sin.
At the same time that you pray with your whole heart,

you remain a sinner with your whole heart (*fortisimus peccator*), and that is why you must believe and pray. The problem, and the unescapable problem of sin, the question of managing to feel free from *sin*, is at the centre of Luther's religious preoccupations. Everything gravitates around that problem. The true notion of grace had always escaped him, so that during the period of his Pelagianism he endeavoured to *make himself* without sin by his own powers, and, after his deliverance, he endeavoured to *feel himself* without sin albeit sinning in all his actions[1] (mortally, inasmuch as for Luther all sin is of itself mortal)[2] and thus to vanquish conscience, mistress of despair. "Est autem maximus labor, posse haec ita fide apprehendere et credere ut dicas: Peccavi et non peccavi ut sic vincatur conscientia potentissima domina, quae saepe ad desperationem, ad gloriam et ad laqueum homines adigit. . . . Neque est Christianismus aliud quam perpetuum hujus loci exercitium, nempe sentire te non habere peccatum, quamvis peccaris, sed peccata tua in Christo haerere, qui est salvator in aeternum a peccato, morte et inferno secundum illud: Agnus Dei, qui tollit peccata mundi" (Opera exeg. lat., XXIII, 141–142, 1532–1534; Weim., XXV, 330, 38–40; 331, 1; 331, 7–16). Why is it ultimately so if not because, as Denifle rightly remarks, our sin, from the moment in which we believe, is wiped out *in him* and not *in us*. "Christianus quasi in alio mundo collocatus, neque peccata, neque merita aliqua habere debet. Quod si peccata se habere sentit, aspiciat ea non qualia sint in sua

---

[1] For Luther all our works are sins because of the corrupt source from which they come; (cf. Ficker, II, 123: "Idcirco enim bene operando peccamus, nisi Deus per Christum nobis hoc imperfectum tegeret et non imputaret . . ."; 332: "Baptizatus at penitens manet in infirmitate concupiscentiae, quae tamen est contra legem—Non concupisces—et utique *mortalis*, nisi Deus misericors non imputaret propter incoeptam curationem.") "Our works of justification are sins," he had already said in his sermon on the 26 December, 1515. (Weim. I, 31, 15.) And again: "All our works are produced in sin, in which we were born." (Weim. I, 190, 1517.) It is the same even for repentance and contrition, in which concupiscence is always mixed.

[2] Cf. Ficker, II, 123; Weim., II, 410.

persona, sed qualia sint in illa persona, in quam a Deo sunt coniecta hoc est, videat qualia sint non in se nec in conscientia sua, sed in Christo, in quo expiata et devicta sunt. . . . Dicas enim: peccata mea non sunt mea, quia non sunt in me, sed sunt aliena, Christi videlicet: non ergo me laedere poterunt" (Opera exeg. lat., XXIII, 141; Weim., XXV, 330, 22–28 and 36–37). "Peccata sua (credentis) jam non sua, sed Christi sunt. At in Christo, peccata justitiam vincere non possunt, sed vincantur, ideo in ipso consumuntur." (Weim., II, 504 [1519].) "Quare fides pure est docenda, quod scilicet *per eam* sic conglutineris Christo, ut ex te et ipso fiat quasi una persona . . . ut cum fiducia dicere possis: Ego sum Christus; hoc est, Christi justitia, victoria, vita, etc., est mea; et vicissim Christus dicat: Ego sum ille peccator, hoc est, ejus peccata, mors, etc., sunt mea, quia adhaeret mihi, et ego illi, conjuncti enim sumus *per fidem* in unam carnem et os." (*Comm. in Galat.*, 1535, Weim., XL, P.I, 285–286.) So that we adhere to Christ, so closely as to become one person with him, through faith alone (not through charity)—by an act of faith and of confidence which co-exists with our radical state of sin and iniquity and with the sins which we go on committing in spite of faith, and which does not bring about in us any real and intrinsic participation in the life and justice of Christ. Now we are back to the *pecca fortiter* of the letter to Melanchthon.[1] "If you have committed all possible sins," says Luther again, "God is not your enemy to the extent that all that will not be effaced and pardoned if you begin to believe. For, through faith Christ becomes your own, He who has been given to you precisely in order to wash away your sins. . . . That is why, if you believe, no sin can remain, however grave. Then you become the beloved child and all sin goes and all that you do is well." (Weim. [1523], XII, 559, 6–12.)

No sin can damn the Christian save only want of faith; as long as he does not lose faith he cannot lose his soul. "Nulla peccata Christianum possunt damnare, nisi sola

[1] Quoted at the beginning of this note.

incredulitas, caetera omnia, redeat vel stet fides in promis-
sionem divinam baptizato factam, in momento absorbentur
per eandem fidem." (Weim., VI, 529 *De captiv. Babylon,*
1530.) In short, "it is enough to acknowledge, through the
riches of God's glory, the Lamb which bears the sins of the
world; sin cannot separate us from Him even should we fall
a thousand times a day into fornication or homicide."

39. "But yes," naïvely exclaims M. Karl Holl (*Rev.
de théol. et de phil.* art. cit.), "Luther, who wrote *De servo
arbitrio* had dwelt long on this question."

Here again M. Karl Holl misses the point completely.
It is not a question of knowing whether "Christ fights
in man against the flesh" or whether our bad inclinations
fight "in us, at the same time, against that sanctifying
power" so that all our refuge lies in the mercy of God.
(Ibid.) What Christian will contest these truths? Can
one find there an original thought, proper to Luther?
Nor is it a question of knowing whether our will brings
much evil into our good intentions: (Ibid.) a thing which
everyone would equally agree to; nor whether in the
presence of one of these actions, taken apart, man dares
say: It is a good work *in the full meaning of the term*, it is a
work *wholly inspired by God.*[1] Who would ever give himself
such an assurance? And is not a mind which even asks such
a question entirely occupied with pharisaical scruples?

We want to know whether, in spite of the forgiveness
of God and the justification which covers us externally,
works, proceeding from human activity, remain substantially bad because proceeding from a source essentially
corrupted;[2] whether the evil which is mixed with our
actions by the act of our own will makes of these actions,
so many sins, of themselves mortal,[3] and lastly whether

---

[1] Ibid.: the italics are ours.

[2] It is this assertion that Bossuet, in the passage quoted, answers
particularly.

[3] It is known that Luther thought the distinction between mortal
and venial sin absurd. In his eyes all sins were of themselves mortal,
and only became venial through the mercy of God. (Cf. *Com. in Ep.
Rom.*, Ficker, II, 123, 332, cf. also Weim., II, 410.)

the works which God produces in us are not simultaneously produced entirely by our own activity. That is what Bossuet reproached Luther with not having understood. That Luther wrote *De servo arbitrio* is certainly no proof that he understood those things. On the contrary, it is the proof that he did not understand anything about it.

DESCARTES

40. Cf. Hannequin: *la Méthode de Descartes*, Rev. de Mét. et de Mor., 1906; Hamelin: *le Système de Descartes*, p. 82. Hamelin writes very justly (p. 87): "Descartes's whole theory of knowledge is, then, summed up in this, that to know is to apprehend by an infallible intuition simple natures and the links of those simple natures, which are themselves simple natures."

41. We know that for Descartes an atheist has not the *certain knowledge* of any truth, for his best established conclusions can always be rendered doubtful by the hypothesis of the evil Genius.

In fact, at the moment when a demonstration makes a conclusion evident to us, we are relying on premises which we hold to be true and have been themselves the subject of demonstration, but which are not so evident as to compel our thoughts at the time, since at the given moment our act of intellection is not brought to bear on them, but on the conclusion in connexion with them. We remember having seen them as true, we do not then see them as true. And as we are not at the time compelled by their obviousness, it is enough for the hypothesis of the evil Genius to occur to our mind and be accepted by us, for a doubt affecting these propositions to become possible.

Descartes, who does not seem to have explicitly made clear the question of the *rightful* value of our faculties of cognition, but to have had chiefly in view to conquer *actually* the state of doubt (of doubt really practised) which he himself created by giving rash welcome to the hypothesis of the evil Genius, Descartes sees only one way of escaping this difficulty. That is, to have recourse to the existence of God and His truthfulness, in order to free himself from the hypothesis of the evil Genius first of all accepted. For him who knows that existence, the hypothesis of the evil Genius has henceforth lost all its sting,—the temptation is overcome,—and from then onwards demonstrated conclusions can no longer be rendered doubtful; that man truly *knows*.

Such is, we think, the true bearing of Cartesian thought here. Does it, even understood in this way, escape the objection of the vicious circle? No; for that truth "God exists," is itself a demonstrated conclusion, and when I am not at the moment under the compelling clearness of the demonstration which establishes it, I am not, in good Cartesian logic, in such a position as not to be subject in this matter to the uncertainty brought by the hypothesis of the evil Genius.

To avoid the vicious circle, it would be necessary to make that conclusion an intuition co-existing with the whole stream of my thought: The ontologism which Descartes would never admit is thus the limit to which Cartesian metaphysic essentially tends, and the only way it can find its balance.

42. Our errors in speculative questions are *contingent* (avoidable), they are not in themselves acts *of our liberty* (for then they would always be moral faults). By basing (cf. Gilson: *La Liberté chez Descartes et la théologie*, p. 266; Gouhier: *la Pensée religieuse de Descartes*, p. 212–215) the theory of error on that of sin, Descartes comes, without daring to admit it clearly to himself, to make all error a moral sin. In reality, when we give our assent to an object which we think to be evident to us without its truly being so, it is by reason of a fault in the discursive process of the intelligence, and that fault does not necessarily depend on the will *in so far as it is free*—that is to say, inasmuch as it relates the judgement of the intelligence with regard to its proper object (the Good of man); it only depends necessarily on the will inasmuch as

the will applies to the work a reason weak at the time (lacking *hic et nunc* the required perspicacity,) and consequently produces adherence to an object insufficiently elucidated.

"There is no error of judgement without sin," writes R. P. Roland-Gosselin in his study *La Théorie Thomiste de l'erreur* (*Mélanges Thomistes*, 1923, p. 266). This thesis, even if one tries to mitigate its consequences, seems to us excessive. Does not St. Thomas teach that even the conscience can make involuntary mistakes (that is to say mistakes not due to a moral fault of the will), which excuse from sin? (*Sum. Theol.* I–II, 19, 6.) Then it will be all the more possible to have speculative mistakes which do not involve any sin (save, of course, in their first principle—the fault through which Adam lost original justice and the preternatural privilege of inerrancy which it implied). If error in its proper nature, in so far as it is a *judgement* upon something *not known*, implies an element of *presumption* (*De Malo* III, 7) yet if we consider the subject, that is the person who is in error, this presumption is formally a sin only to him who knows that he does *not know*, otherwise it remains material.

43. See the theory of mode outlined in the *Principes*, first Part, art. 64 and 65. Cf. Letter to X . . ., 1645 or 1646, A.—T., IV, 348—349. The distinction between substance and mode has a real foundation for Descartes: in that sense it can be called real (minor real), and it differs from simple distinction of reason (*rationis ratiocinatae*), cf. Roland-Gosselin: *Revue des sciences philosophiques et théol.*, 1910, p. 306–307.

But above all, the important point is that in his thought the distinction between substance and mode (which takes the place henceforth of that between substance and accident) seems to be based upon the scholastic distinction between *substance* and *substantial mode*.

On the historical origins of Cartesian innatism, M. Gilson's study, *L'innéisme cartésien et la théologie* (Études de philosophie médiévale, Strasbourg, 1921) may usefully be consulted.

44. Cf. the author's study on *l'Esprit de Descartes*, "les lettres," 1st February, 1922.

45. Descartes thought that "the single resolve to get rid of all the opinions which one formerly believed is not an example which everyone should follow" (*Disc.*, 2nd Part, A.—T., VI, 14—15), and that for "weak minds" the metaphysical experience of universal doubt, a necessary but dangerous introduction to true philosophy, might turn out badly (to Mersenne, March, 1637, A.—T., I, 349—350; cf. letter to X . . . , I., 353—354; letter to P. Vatier, February, 1638, I, 560). Still he himself made that experiment once for all, devoting himself for us to the combat against the evil Genius; everyone, guided by him and using the precautions indicated in the first *Méditation*, will henceforth be able to gather the benefits of preliminary doubt without experiencing its perils; and so he does not hesitate to have the *Méditations* translated into the common speech and distribute them amongst the public, although he there gave the reasons for doubting all the developments from which, out of prudence, he abstained in the *Discours de la Méthode*.

On the other hand, IN PRACTICE, he quite admitted that all minds are not equally apt for metaphysical speculations (to Mersenne, 27 May, 1638, II, 144—145; 16 October, 1639, II, 597; 13 November, 1639, II, 622, etc.), and that science requires a special gift, perfected by exercise: "Ea (sc. Scientia mathematica) non ex libris, sed ex ipso usu et arte hauriri debet. . . . Omnes autem homines ad eam apti non sunt, sed requiritur ad id ingenium mathematicum, quodque usu poliri debet." (Conversation with Burman, 16 April, 1648; A.—T., V, 176.)

But those were statements to which he was forced, in fact, by experience; and IN THEORY he proceeded in a different sense. In Descartes' *doctrine, natural light suffices*, with method, for the search for truth, "common sense is the best divided thing in the world," "naturally equal in all men," "entire in each" (*Disc.*, 1st Part, A.—T., VI, 1, 2), only it is advisable to free oneself from prejudices which obscure it;[1] and the idea of the Method is to lead man, by the resources of common sense alone, as they are found "even in those who have not studied," to a "universal science" which will raise our nature "to its highest degree of perfection." (Cf. the early title of the *Discours*.)

Cartesian innatism, the negation of the reality of accidents and qualities, the theory of understanding and clear ideas, everything which is deepest in Descartes' thought, involves an absolute refusal to admit the qualities intrinsically perfecting the intellect and adapting it to a special object, which Scholasticism called *habitus*. If Descartes recognizes natural inequalities in understandings, he entirely fails to recognize the differences and inequalities due to the development of these spiritual qualities (which are quite a different thing from simple habit or exercise). It is the very opposite of an "aristocratic metaphysic." (M. Henri Gouhier: *Pensée religieuse de Descartes*, p. 300-307, seems here to have adopted much too superficial a view.)

46. Cf. *Principes*, 1st Part, art. 58 and 59.

47. Cf. M.-D. Roland-Gosselin: "La Révolution cartésienne," *Revue des sciences philos. et théol.*, 1910, p. 678—693.

48. The most decisive, but the longest way of revealing the theory of representational ideas in Descartes is to show the essential part played by that theory in the great theses of Cartesian metaphysics. As to the passages of the philosopher bearing on the nature of thought and ideas, if they are often doubtful, yet certain of them clearly express that theory. We will quote some of them here:

1st. Descartes writes in the *Abrégé*, the sequel to the *Réponses aux secondes Objections*: "By the word 'thought'

[1] What metaphysical meditations require is a "mind entirely free from all prejudice and able easily to detach itself from the business of the senses" (Dedicatory epistle to the *Méditations*, A.—T., IX, 7), that is to say, a mind freed from the *impediments* which stand in the way of its *nature*.

I understand everything which is in us in such a way
that we are immediately conscious of it (the Latin
text is: ut ejus immediate conscii simus). Thus
all the operations of the will, the understanding, the
imagination, and the senses, are thoughts." (A.—T.,
VII, 160; IX, 124.) And in the *Principes* I, 9: "By the
word 'thought' I mean everything that takes place in
us in such a way that we perceive it immediately by
ourselves (quae nobis consciis in nobis fiunt, quatenus
eorum in nobis conscientia est); that is why not only
understanding, willing, imagining, but also feeling, are
the same thing as thinking."

Thus thought is defined by consciousness—(let us say
more strictly that consciousness, which, at least in virtue
of being concomitant consciousness, *in actu exercito*, is
indeed a *property* of thought, but not its essence, now
becomes its formal constituent); and in consequence *feeling*
and *understanding* in themselves no more overpass the sphere
of consciousness of oneself than *willing* and *imagining*, and
equally only "pose" the subject for himself.[1]

On the other hand, and by definition, thought itself
is the sole object which it "immediately perceives" and
ideas make us know immediately not things, nor natures,
but our thought: "By the name 'idea' I mean that
form of each of our thoughts, by the immediate perception
of which I am cognizant of *those same thoughts*, per cujus
immediatam perceptionem ipsius ejusdem cogitationis
conscius sum." (A.—T., VII, 160: IX, 124.)

2nd. *Principes*, I, 13. Our thought "finds in itself
first the *ideas* of several things; and so long as it *contemplates them simply*, and does not affirm that there is nothing
outside itself which is like these ideas, and also does not
deny it, it is in no danger of making a mistake."

Thus what is *contemplated*, what is the object of apprehension, is the *ideas* themselves; and truth, which was for
the ancients the harmony, with extramental being, of *mental
composition* between two objects of thought, that is to say
between two quiddities, becomes the resemblance of such

[1] Cf. Hamelin: *le Systéme de Descartes*, p. 181.

an object of thought, that is to say now, of such an *idea*, with an extra-mental thing ("ideate", Spinoza called it): a confusion of capital importance, which will vitiate all post-Cartesian speculation, on Spinoza's side as well as Hume's.

3rd. We know that for Descartes not only is the production of an image a pre-requisite to the perception of the external sense, as Suarez taught against St. Thomas ("idea" in Cartesian language, "species expressa" in that of the Scholastics), but moreover that perception has as term immediately attained (*object quod*) only the (confused) idea itself, the sensible affection, which represents no extra-mental reality like itself.[1]

But it is exactly on the same type that Descartes pictures sensation and intellection, with this difference, that in the case of the sensible qualities *there is no resemblance* between the actually existent thing and the idea (essentially confused, not expressible in a purely rational definition), whilst in the case of intelligible objects *there is resemblance* between the thing actually or possibly existing and the idea (clear and distinct). In both cases it is not *what is* (a concrete thing grasped in itself by the sense, or an abstract quiddity grasped in a concept by the intelligence), it is the *idea* which is the object first grasped, the object immediately presented to the mind.

4th. *Troisième Méditation:* "But considering them (the ideas) as images, of which some represent one thing and some another, it is evident that they are very different from one another. For, in fact, those which represent substances to me are without doubt something more, and contain in themselves, so to speak, more objective reality, that is to say participate by representation in more degrees of being or perfection, than those which represent to me only modes or accidents." What does Descartes mean here by "objective reality" of ideas? Is it the thing

[1] Cf. *Principia philosophiæ*, I, 66–71. "There is nothing more conformed to reason than to believe that the spirit newly united to the body of a child is only busied with *feeling or perceiving confusedly* THE IDEAS of pain, tickling, warmth, cold, and the like . . . (to Mersenne, 25th July, 1641).

itself as known, the intelligible nature itself in so far as it is presented, *objectivized* to the mind by the idea? No, it is a certain quality of the idea itself, it is the degree of perfection of the idea taken as the object first known making an ideate to be known, as an instrumental sign or portrait.[1]

The proof of this is that he seeks the cause of the degree of "objective reality" contained in his ideas, applying to the "objective reality" of ideas the principle: "There must be as much reality in the efficient and total cause as in its effect." (A.—T., IX, 31-32.)

Thus the immediate objects of our apprehension (what he calls the "objective reality" of ideas), what is first known in every act of cognition, are *effects caused in our thought*, which resemble things. The thing is an object No. 2 placed behind the object No. 1, which that object No. 1, which is the idea itself, resembled (by the institution of a God who cannot deceive us).

5th. *Réponses aux premières Objections :* "I am speaking of the *idea* which is never outside the understanding, and in respect of which to be objectively means nothing else than to be in the understanding *in the way in which objects are accustomed to be in it*." (IX, 82.) It would be impossible to say more clearly that the immediate *object* of the understanding is the *idea* itself.

To that should be added the theory of *materially false* ideas in which Descartes confuses and applies wrongly two theories which were classical in the School (that of the intelligence erring *per accidens* when it composes a definition with incompossible notes, and that of the being of reason). A materially false idea is a false portrait, a true idea is a true portrait: in both it is the portrait which is the object first attained by the intelligence.

---

[1] Cf. ibid.: "So that natural light makes me know evidently that *the ideas are in me as representations or images,* which may in truth easily fall from the perfection of the things from which they have been drawn, but which can never contain anything greater and more perfect." (IX, 33.) The whole Cartesian demonstration clearly shows that it is a question there of images or representations *first seen themselves, and* not of images (formal signs) by which *something else is seen.*

When Locke enunciates as a truth of immediate experience: that since the mind has no other object of its
thoughts and reasonings than its own ideas, which are
the only thing it contemplates or can contemplate, it
is evident that all our knowledge turns only on our ideas,
(Essay, Book IV, ch. 1), he shows himself a logical
Cartesian. More generally one can say that the whole
controversy about ideas which occupied the end of the
seventeenth century depends on the Cartesian notion of
representation-ideas. (We were pleased to find in the
Commentaire of M. Etienne Gilson on the Discours de la
Méthode (Paris, Vrin, 1923, in particular pp. 318-323)
a confirmation of the interpretation here expounded of
the Cartesian ideas, of their rôle as portraits and of
their relation to the "idées factives" of the creator.)
Among the numerous texts quoted by M. Gilson let
us note the following which we had not mentioned:
"Atqui ego passim ubique ac praecipue hoc ipso in
loco ostendo me nomen ideae sumere pro omni eo
quod immediate a mente percipitur. . . . Ususque
sum hoc nomine, quia jam tritum erat a philosophis
ad formas perceptionum mentis divinae significandas
quamvis nullam in Deo phantasiam agnoscamus;
et nullum aptius habebam" (III ce Resp. A—T., VII,
181).

In the Réflexions sur l'intelligence we had indicated that
line of descent which seems to connect, on this point, the
ideology of Descartes with that of Vasquez. As M. Roland
Dalbiez has recently shown the comparison with the
Scotist theory of ideas—which attributes to the esse
cognitum as such a sort of existence (esse diminutum) intermediary between real being and the being of reason—
seems no less suggestive (cf. Cajetan in I, 14, 5 and in
I, 15, 1).

49. Conversation with Burman, A.—T., V, p. 157.
Descartes' answers to Burman, who points out to him
that the idea of the angel, which is dealt with amongst
other things in the third Méditation, cannot differ from the

idea of our mind, *cum utraque sit res solum cogitans*, are curious to note. They show that he has no idea of metaphysical analogy: from the notion of our spirit we cannot, according to him, draw out anything concerning pure spirit—an agnosticism which must apply with still more reason to the infinite Spirit. It is true that Descartes holds that we have a direct idea of God, "the clearest and most distinct" of all our ideas. He thus avoids agnosticism only by opening the door to ontologism.

50. "Ut comoedi, moniti ne in fronte appareat pudorpersonam induunt; sic ego, hoc mundi theatrum cons scensurus, in quo hactenus spectator exstiti, larvatu, prodeo." Whatever the literal meaning (a little weakened, it seems, by MM. Milhaud and Gouhier) of these lines written by Descartes at the age of twenty-three may be, they have, as regards the philosopher's work, a most striking symbolic significance, and one that is most exact.

These lines, preceded in Leibnitz's manuscript copy (published by Foucher de Careil, and itself lost) by the note: "1619. Calendis Januarii", are taken from a youthful manuscript now lost, and appear, at least at first sight, to belong to January, 1619.

Yet Baillet writes of the *Parnassus* (A.—T., X, 213, note b.): "Mr. Borel thought that it was a book composed in 1619, dated the first of January, which M. Descartes put at the top of the Register. But it may happen that the date was only for the blank register and that it meant nothing except that M. Descartes began to use that Register on the 1st of January, 1619." Baillet adds in the margin with respect to the title *Parnassus*: "Pierre Roten, whom M. Descartes did not know until the following year in Germany, is mentioned in it; but perhaps that is a later addition."

It is more likely that Descartes inscribed the date 1st January, 1619, at the top of the Register which he meant to use, but wrote only later the notes which compose the *Parnassus*. Also we are inclined to believe that the lines quoted above were not written before, but after the dream in which Descartes' mission was revealed to him, that is to say after 10th December, 1619. On Descartes' dream see G. Milhaud's study (*Une crise mystique chez Descartes en 1619*, Revue de Mét. et de Mor., July, 1916) and our study in the *Revue Universelle* (*le Songe de Descartes*, 1st December, 1920).

51. Some notes on the naturalist tendencies of Cartesian philosophy will be found in our study, *l'Esprit de Descartes* (les Lettres, 1st March, 1922, p. 416ff.).

As regards the theological repercussions of Cartesian metaphysic, let us quote here the important observations of Fr. Bainvel (*Nature et Surnaturel*, p. 73): "The super-natural and divine gifts are something real and physical: on the other hand, they are not the substance of the soul, but something added, something inherent in the soul; in short, they were conceived as accidents, as qualities. . . . Descartes came, and it is well known what a war he and his followers waged against these scholastic entities, these accidents, these qualities, which do not correspond with any 'clear and distinct' idea. There must no longer be anything but substances. What will come of the supernatural accidents in the storm? . . . In fact, the new theology, emancipated from scholasticism, at last almost forgot, in the eighteenth century, and a good part of the nineteenth, sanctifying grace and the supernatural gifts. Sin and grace were no longer considered as any-thing but moral denominations corresponding with ideas of philosophic and natural integrity. It was . . . to suppress the reality of the supernatural and keep only the word. These ideas were current for a long time, notably in France and in Germany."

ROUSSEAU

52. Cf. *Confess.*, Book III: "Two almost incompatible things are joined together in me, I cannot conceive how: a very ardent disposition, very impetuous passions, and ideas which come slowly and indistinctly, and never present

themselves until it is too late. You would say that my heart and my mind did not belong to the same individual. Feeling fills my soul more quickly than a flash of lightning; but instead of enlightening me it burns and dazzles me. I feel everything and see nothing. I am passionate, but stupid; I must be cool to think.

"I have that slowness of thought with that quickness of feeling not only in conversation, but even by myself and when I am working. My ideas get into order in my head with the most incredible difficulty; they go round in it secretly, they work in it until they excite me, inflame me, give me palpitations; and amidst all this emotion I see nothing clearly, I could not write a single word, I must wait. . . . Imperceptibly that great movement quietens down, that chaos clears, everything falls into its place, but slowly, and after long and confused agitation. . . ."

Second Dialogue: "In a word, I have almost always found him laborious in thought, awkward in speech, ever wearied with looking for the right word which never comes, and confusing ideas which were already none too clear by bad expression of them."

Letter to Dom Deschamps, 12th September, 1762 (Masson, II, 84): "It is good of you to scold me for the inaccuracy of my reasoning. Have you at last discovered that I see certain objects very well but that I cannot compare them, that I am quite fertile in propositions without ever seeing consequences, that order and method, which are your gods, are my furies; that nothing ever presents itself to me except in isolation, and that instead of linking my ideas in letters I employ a mental sleight of hand, which particularly impresses all you great philosophers? That is the reason why I have started to despise you, as I see well that I could not catch up with you." No doubt there is some irony in these admissions, but at bottom they are sincere, as M. Masson rightly observes.

53. On the Thomist doctrine of the acts of the practical intelligence and the will, see the masterly and penetrating

analyses of Fr. Gardeil, particularly in his study on *le Gouvernement de soi-même* (*Revue thomiste*, April-June, 1918).

54. Cf. *Second Dialogue :* "Sometimes, inflamed by long contemplation of an object, he forms strong and ready resolves which he forgets or gives up before he gets into the street. *All the strength of his will is exhausted in resolving ; he has none left to carry out.*"

55. We know that in the *Dialogues*, written between 1772 and 1775, in which we see *Rousseau as the judge of Jean-Jacques*, he relates that in his solitary walks he created for himself a whole band of romantic phantoms amongst whom he lived, with whom he talked, who made for him a world more real than the world of earth. That is a very curious phenomenon of mental discharge, in which imaginative play comes near to hallucination. The psychology of these singular beings, whom Jean-Jacques calls *our inhabitants*, is in the highest degree instructive for the psychology of Jean-Jacques himself. I will merely point out certain characteristics here.

"It is just their ardour"—he is speaking of *our inhabitants*—"which keeps them inactive. The celestial state for which they long, which is their primary need by the strength with which it presents itself to their hearts, makes them collect and stretch out all the powers of their soul to come to it. The obstacles which keep them back could not so occupy them as to make them forget it for a moment; and from that comes that mortal disgust for everything else and that total inactivity when they despair of reaching the only object of their desires. . . .

"Perhaps in those lands people are not more virtuous than in our parts, but they love virtue better. As the true inclinations of nature are all good, by surrendering to them they are good themselves; but amongst us virtue often obliges us to fight and conquer nature and they are rarely capable of such efforts. Long want of habit of resisting may even enervate their souls until they do evil out of weakness, fear, or necessity. They are not exempt from faults or vices; even crime is not foreign to them, since there are deplorable situations in which the highest virtue hardly suffices to keep one from it, and which drive to evil the man who is weak in spite of his heart: but the express will to harm, envenomed hatred, envy, baseness, treachery, trickery are unknown there; too often are the guilty seen there, never is a wicked person seen. . . .

"They are also less active, or rather, less restless. Their efforts to attain the object which they contemplate consist in strong transports; but as soon as they feel their powerlessness they stop, without looking for equivalents of that unique object, which alone can tempt them, within their range. . . ." *First Dialogue :* Cf. also *Rêveries,* 8th Promenade. There would be a whole study to make besides on *Jean-Jacques and dreaming* in which it would be necessary to take account not only of the *Rêveries* and the *Dialogues* but also of *Émile* and the *Contrat Social* (cf. above p. 135, 136) and there one could show in Rousseau an authentic forerunner of the *super-realism* which recently filled the literary stage.

"Never did man," writes Jean-Jacques again of himself, "act less on principles and rules, or follow his inclinations more blindly. Prudence, reason, caution, foresight, all those are words of no account for him. When he is tempted, he yields; when he is not, he remains languid. By that you see that his behaviour cannot but be unequal and erratic, at times impetuous, and almost always nerveless or ineffectual. He does not walk; he leaps and falls back where he was; even his activity tends only to bring him back to that from which force of circumstances draws him; and if he were not driven by his most constant desire, he would be ever motionless. In short, there never was a being more sensitive to emotion and less framed for action." *Second Dialogue.*

In a letter (not sent) to the Marquis de Mirabeau (March, 1767) he was already saying: "My philosophy? Oh, My Lord Marquis, you do me an honour which I hardly deserve. Systems of all kinds are beyond me; I have none in my life and behaviour. It is no longer my business to reflect, compare, quibble, persist, fight; I give myself up to the impression of the moment without resistance and even without scruple; for I am perfectly certain that my heart only loves what is good. All the evil that I have done in my life, I have done by reflection, and what little good I have been able to do, I have done on impulse." (*Revue de Paris*, 15th September, 1923, unpublished letters of J.-J.R., collected by Théophile Dufour.)

56. On the psychosis of Rousseau and the essential part it played in his life and work, it will be of interest to read the studies of M. Victor Demole: "Analyse psychiatrique des Confessions" (*Archives Suisses de Neurologie et de Psychiatrie*, no. 2, vol. II, 1918), and "Rôle du tempérament et des idées délirantes de Rousseau dans la genése de ses principales théories" (*Annales médico-psychologiques*, January, 1922).

The author thinks that in Rousseau "far from hampering literary genius, illness constantly favoured it" (Annales, p. 19). Let us quote his conclusions: "To sum up, Rousseau's mental sickness in great measure determined his activity: (1) some symptoms forming an integrant part of his character (exalted emotionalism, negativism, ambivalence, impulsiveness, sexual anomalies, etc.) furnished a considerable number of advantageous or disadvantageous elements which the writer turned to account. Negativism and ambivalence especially, by producing disagreeable social situations, increased dissatisfaction, excited egoism, and forced Rousseau to isolate himself in nature; (2) Rousseau's egoism gave him his direction in the speculative sphere in which he triumphs. Some works are the direct transcription of the dreams in which he realized his desires (*Nouvelle Héloïse*). (3) Rousseau's dissociation allowed him to cultivate a high ideal whilst living in the midst of debauchery and claim a certificate for virtue in despite of the evidence; without that inconsequence several of his works would never have appeared; (4) Rousseau's pride and his experience as a paranoiac contributed to cause him to accept the fundamental idea of the perfection of nature of which his other theses are corollaries; (5) Rousseau's intellectual output is evidently correlative to his psychosis; his delirium about persecution suddenly excited him and compelled him to write in self-defence . . ." (Ibid., p. 34).

A Freudian psychologist really ought to give us a work on the *Confessions* also. It is for such cases as that that the themes of psycho-analysis are made. Yet we must not forget that in an intelligence of so high a natural quality illness only sets in relief and betrays, so to say, in the pure state the logic of certain principles.

The final psychological fissure of which we have spoken seems to have come about in 1749 (the year of the *Discours sur les sciences et les arts*). That period saw the simultaneous manifestation in Rousseau (he was then thirty-seven) of literary genius and mental sickness properly so called. The latter was soon manifested by the crisis of exaltation and "renunciation of the world" to which we have alluded. "The systematization of a delirium and a maniacal excitement" had been needed "to co-ordinate his efforts at last." (Victor Demole, loc. cit., p. 27.)

57. Cf. *Confess.*, Book IX. "Up till then I had been good: from thenceforth I became virtuous, or at least intoxicated with virtue. That intoxication began in my head, but it passed into my heart. The noblest pride sprang up there on the remains of uprooted vanity. This was not make-believe: I actually became what I appeared; and for the four years at least that the effervescence lasted in full strength, nothing great and beautiful could enter a human heart of which I was not capable between heaven and myself. That was where my sudden eloquence was born, that was the source of that truly celestial fire which suffused my first books and inflamed me, not the smallest spark of which had made its way out for forty years because it was not yet kindled.

"I was truly transformed; my friends and acquaintances no longer recognized me. No longer was I the timid man, rather shamefaced than modest, who did not dare come forward or speak; who was put out by a chaffing word and blushed at a word from a woman. Bold, spirited, intrepid, I showed everywhere an assurance which was the firmer that it was simple and lay more in my soul than in my bearing. The contempt which my deep meditations had given me for the habits, maxims, and prejudices of my age, made me insensible to the jeers of those who had them, and I smashed their little witticisms with my sentences as I should smash an insect between my fingers. What a change! All Paris was repeating the sharp and biting sarcasms of that same man who two years before and ten years afterwards never knew what he ought to say nor what words to use."

"Since then my soul has been swinging to and fro across the line of rest and its ever renewed oscillations have never suffered it to remain there . . . a terrible time in a lot without precedent in mortal man."

58. "He adds that he cannot disguise from me, or from himself, that it was an attack of madness." Corancez, *de J.-J. Rousseau*, p. 49.

59. Cf. Lévy-Bruhl: *La querelle de Hume et de Rousseau* (Rev. de mét. et de morale, May, 1912).

60. There was the same enthusiasm in Germany. Herder invokes Jean-Jacques in passionate terms: "It is myself I want to look for, to find myself at last, and lose myself no more; come, Rousseau! And be my guide." His fiancée, Caroline, considers Rousseau "a saint and a prophet" whom she adores. Campe engraves on the pedestal of a statue of Jean-Jacques the words: "To my saint. . . ." (On Rousseau's influence in Germany, see J. Texte: *J.-J. Rousseau et le cosmopolitisme littéraire*. Paris 1909, and L. Reynaud: *Hist. de l'influence française en Allemagne, Paris*, 1914.)

61. In the fourth book of Émile, under the pretext that self-love is the primitive passion—which is true, but does

not prevent love of the Source of our being from being yet more primitive, or prevent every creature from loving naturally more than itself Him "from Whom it is according to all that it is" *cujus est, secundum hoc ipsum, quod est,* "otherwise natural love would be perverse and would not be completed but destroyed by charity," *Summa Theol.,* I, 60, 5—Rousseau was already explaining that we ought to love ourselves *more than anything,* and distinguishing between the "self esteem" which compares itself with others and, being engendered by the life of intercourse, produces hateful passions, and the "love of self" which is concerned only with ourselves in the solitude of our absolute Self, and is the source of all kindness. In short, he was already making love of self a substitute for love of God, and thus outlining even at that time a projection in theory of his own psychology which had not yet come to its full pathological evolution.

With that he was persuaded that he was utterly innocent of egoism and depicted himself as "only seeking his own happiness in that of others." (Letter to M. Perdriau, 28th September, 1754. *Corresp. générale* published by Théoph. Dufour, vol. II, p. 132.)

62. *Rêveries,* First Promenade. Cf. Sixth Promenade: "If my face and features were as completely unknown to men as are my character and disposition I should still live among them without grief . . . freely given over to my natural inclinations, I should love them although they never troubled about me. I should exercise a universal and perfectly disinterested good will over them . . . if I had remained free, hidden, isolated, I should have done nothing but good. . . . *If I had been invisible and omnipotent like God, I should have been beneficent and good as He is.*"

63. There is such lamentable misuse of the word "mysticism" in our days, that it is the more important to recover and settle its exact meaning.

There are two methods of definition: one, which can be called material, or by the greatest extension, and is that of the moderns; and a method which we shall call formal, or by the purest instance, which was that of the ancients.

By the former, we enclose at a stroke the wide territory which is found actually to belong to a word taken in its crude state, with all the extension it allows in current usage; and we thus risk taking in the oddest elements, as happened to William James when he studied religious experience. By the second, we consider first the most eminent and most typical case in which the word in question is used strictly, to discover particularly the intelligible form which it signifies; then we progressively widen the sense thus obtained, extending the notion, stretching it to the extreme limit of elasticity.

If we use the second method and question the science competent in the matter, I mean, theology, we see that the word mysticism belongs strictly and primarily to the "experimental knowledge of divine things obtained by the gift of Wisdom," and more generally to the state of the man who lives habitually "under the governance of the gifts of the Holy Spirit." That is the perfectly accurate notion of mysticism; it is a life which is at the same time intellectual and affective, and super-eminently so, since the gift of Wisdom, if it supposes charity, resides in the intelligence. The mystic is beyond reason—because he is united to the source of reason, intelligence in him becomes the disciple of love—because, deprived on earth of the vision of God, charity alone can connaturalize us with divine things and so obtain for us a super-rational knowledge of those things.

How will that essentially theological notion expand by becoming debased?

Make it fall to the level of nature, and it will then mean every effort to arrive at divine union or some substitute for it (the Absolute, Truth, Perfection, Power. . . .) by overpassing reason, but by natural means. It may be by feeling and then we have the mysticism of sensibility, "belphegorism," to use a fashionable word; it may be by pure intelligence, and then we have the mysticism of the intelligence, we may say, in a very general sense, the

Gnosis, or that kind of metaphysical ecstasy of which there seem to be traces in the Upanishads.

Lastly, if the notion of mysticism gets still more degraded and lowered, the word mystic will be applied to the state of anyone who is guided not by reason, but by a semi-religious "faith" in any ideal (or myth), and in this sense Péguy spoke of republican mysticism; yet more generally the term will be applied to the state of a man naturally disposed to admit the existence of an invisible world of greater importance for us than the visible world, and to seek in things an element which simple rational knowledge is inadequate to grasp.

We can collect thus, although distinguishing their worth and degrees, most of the acceptations of the word mystic which are used at the present time, but we also see that all these secondary acceptations are increasingly inaccurate as they get away from the typical sense; a notion which relates to the full possession of the soul by the Holy Spirit, to a state which is not only *above* reason, but essentially supernatural, cannot be extended except by exterior analogies to the states of metaphysical concentration which at their highest could never do more than brush the natural intellectuality of pure spirits, and *a fortiori* to the allusions which, out of ambition, or resignation of the intelligence, lower man *beneath* reason, or to simple natural dispositions to sympathize with mystery. .

"Nearly a century ago," writes M. Seillière, "Ballanche placed him (Rousseau) among the great mystics resulting from the preaching of Jesus, in the train of Dante and St. Teresa." That is nearly as accurate as to place the marmoset among the great human beings resulting from the creative act, in the train of Abraham and Booz.

64. *Second Dialogue.* Listen to this admission by the author of Émile. "I have said that Jean-Jacques was not virtuous: nor would our man be virtuous; and how could he be, weak and subjugated by his inclinations, having his own heart as his guide always, and never his duty or his reason? How could virtue, which is all labour and

struggle, live in the midst of slackness and sweet idleness? He would be good, because nature would have made him so; he would do good, because it would be pleasant to him to do it; but if it were a question of fighting his dearest desires and lacerating his heart to fulfil his duty, would he do that too? I doubt it. *The law of nature, or at least the voice of nature, does not go as far as that.* Then another must command, and nature must be silent. But would he put himself in those violent situations from which such cruel duties arise? I doubt that even more. . . ."

65. The following passage which belongs to 1769, appears to me to illuminate most interestingly the genesis of these pseudo-mystical ideas. It shows very clearly with what strongly felt but soon wrested truths the slipping began: "Always in good faith with myself, I feel joined to my reasonings, however simple, the weight of interior assent. You think that this should be distrusted; I could not think as you do about this, and I, on the contrary, find in that inmost judgement a natural safeguard against the sophisms of my reason. I even fear that you are, in that, confusing the secret inclinations of our heart which lead us astray with the more secret dictates which are even more interior, and protest and murmur against those selfish decisions, and bring us back to the way of truth despite ourselves. That interior feeling is that of nature herself, it is an appeal from her against the sophisms of reason; and the proof of that is, that it never speaks more loudly than when our will is yielding with more compliance to the judgments which it persists in rejecting. Far from believing that he who judges according to that is liable to be deceived, I think that it never deceives us, and that it is the light of our feeble understanding when we want to go beyond what we can conceive." (Letter to M. X. . . ., from Bourgoin, 15th January, 1769.)

Cf. Letter to the Marquis de Mirabeau (not sent), March, 1767: "I am absolutely sure that my heart only loves what is good." (*Rev. de Paris*, 15th September, 1923.)

66. Cf. Frédéric Lefèvre, Interview with C.-F. Ramuz. (*Une heure avec.* . . . 2nd Series, Paris, 1924.)

67. Social life has the solitary life not for its specific end but for its higher limit. The human city has produced its highest results when it is crowned by the contemplative solitude of a certain number of souls united to God, who in their turn, moved by love, intercede for the multitude, and whose wisdom guides the life of that multitude from above.

Let us here remark, following St. Thomas, "that wisdom, i.e. the knowledge of divine things, is one thing for Christians, another for non-Christian philosophers: for we know that our life has for its end the fruition of God Himself, and is diverted towards that end according to a certain participation in the divine nature, which is brought about by grace; wisdom, for us is, therefore, not considered only as a speculation which enables one to know God, as was the case for the philsophers, but also in so far as it has a directing influence on human life, which is not directed solely according to human reason and human rules but also according to divine reason and divine rules, as stated by St. Augustine." In short, and because human life itself participates through sanctifying grace in the order of divine things, wisdom for Christians does not stop, as did the wisdom of philosophers and pagans, in the theoretical knowledge of God: it is at the same time speculative and eminently practical, issues in action and rules our life.

68. In three dissertations of great interest (*Origine des idées politiques de Rousseau*, extracted from the Bulletin de l'Institut genevois, vols. XXIII-XXV, Geneva, 1878, 1881, 1882) M. Jules Vuy showed that in constructing his political theories Rousseau was thinking especially, if not solely, of his native land and the political position of Geneva at the time when he was writing (indeed he himself expressly envisages the condition of a *little* country —not more extensive than a Swiss canton) and that the origin of his dogmas, particularly of the dogma of the

sovereignty of the people, should not be sought in the model
which he had under his eyes in Calvinist Geneva, but on
the contrary, in the memory of episcopal Geneva and her
liberties—of the privileges promulgated by the prince-
bishop Adémar Fabri—often refracted and idealized in
the mind of a furious theorist, sustaining against the
magistrates of the Little Council the claims of the two
privileged classes, citizens and burghers.

It is curious to note with M. Jules Vuy that the name
"citizen," to which the French Revolution was to give
for ever the democratic sense which we know, actually
indicated at Geneva an aristocratic title of which the
"citizen of Geneva" was fully aware and proud before
being led to renounce it by persecution.

69. In M. Seillière's *Jean-Jacques Rousseau* there is an
interesting picture of the variations of Jean-Jacques on
this subject. But it seems that M. Seillière himself ought
to have gone more deeply into the philosophical and
theological meaning of the idea of nature. Without that
one can no 'more usefully study Rousseauism in the
eighteenth century than Jansenism in the seventeenth.

70. From the point of view of historical filiations, the
Rousseauist idea of Natural Goodness doubtless depends
on the great current of naturalism flowing from the
Renaissance and the Cartesian Reformation, but in a
very general way, and especially in the measure in which
it prepared the corruption of Christian dogma. Its true
origins should be sought not only in the theory of the
good savage invented by the imprudent apologetic of the
missionaries of the eighteenth century, but also and much
more thoroughly on one side, in the naturalization of the
very idea of grace which we see develop in the school of
Fénelon (cf. Seillière: *Fénelon et Mme Guyon précurseurs
de J.-J.R.*), on another side, as we have shown elsewhere
(*Réflexions sur l'Intelligence*, ch. IX) in *Jansenism* and
Protestantism, in that heretical exaggeration of pessimism
which so many historians go on taking for the Christian spirit,

and which caused the privileges of the state of innocence to be regarded as due to human nature before it was *essentially corrupted* by original sin.

71. Rightly understood, this truth means: 1. that the *actual state* in which man was created was a state of innocence, integrity, and happiness—that was a *gratuitous and supernatural privilege*, the first pledge of the destiny reserved for us; 2. that *human nature* considered metaphysically, in its essence and first inclinations, is good and directed towards the good, so that the whole work of the reason and culture should, under penalty of the worst havoc, develop along natural lines—that is, as it were, the first stratum of human life. Rousseau's attacks on *modern* society, deeply spoiled by what is artificial and by conditions of life which are contrary to nature, are only too well justified from this point of view, and a certain intelligent naturalism in the fundamental regimen and the hygiene of individuals and societies (cf. the remarkable labours of Doctor Carton) here appears as a more and more necessary reaction.

But all that does not prevent the weakness of human nature; nor the wounds left by original sin; it does not prevent the *nature of each one*, considered concretely and in the individual, being full, in fact, of ferments of disorder and constantly threatened by the "seat of concupiscence" present in it. Far from "all our first inclinations being legitimate,"[1] the will of each man left to the powers of nature alone is, in the state of fallen nature, incapable of efficaciously choosing God as his

[1] "Even in the state of humiliation in which we are during this life, all our first inclinations are legitimate." Émile, Book IV (Profession of faith). The questionable thing is the word "first" which Rousseau understands not only of *metaphysically* fundamental inclinations (in which case his proposition would be true), but also of the *empirically* first movements, that is to say, those anterior to reflexion and rising spontaneously in each from his innermost and most secret heart. Cf. Letter to M. de Beaumont: "The first movements of nature are always righteous." *First Dialogue:* "All the first movements of nature are good and righteous." *Nouvelle Héloïse*, V Part, Letter III. "There is no error in nature."

last end. Grace is needed for that. (Cf. *Summa Theol.*, I—II, 89, 6; 109, 3 and 4.)

72. On Rousseau's philosophical faith, cf. his letter to Voltaire of 18th August, 1756: "As for me, I will confess frankly that neither the *for* nor the *against* seems to me demonstrated on this point by the light of reason alone, and that if the theist only grounds his opinion on probabilities, the atheist, still less precise, appears to me to found his own only on contrary possibilities. Moreover the objections on each side are always insoluble because they turn on things of which men have no true idea. I admit all that, and yet I believe in God as strongly as I believe any other truth, because belief and unbelief are the things which depend least on me; because the state of doubt is a state too violent for my soul; because when my reason drifts my faith cannot remain long in suspense, and resolves without it; because finally a thousand preferences win me over to the most consoling side and add the weight of hope to the balance of reason.

" . . . I do not forbid people to call *prejudice* what I call *proof by feeling*, and I do not hold out that obstinacy of belief as a model; but with perhaps unexampled good faith I give it as an invincible disposition of my soul which nothing will ever be able to overcome, of which I have no complaint so far, and which cannot be attacked without cruelty." (*Corresp. générale*, published by Théophile Dufour, vol. II, p. 319—320.)

73. Cf. *Second Dialogue* : "Pleasing fictions take the place of real happiness with him; and what am I saying? *He alone is firmly happy* since earthly goods may escape him who thinks he holds them, in a thousand ways; *but nothing can take the goods of the imagination from anyone who knows how to enjoy them;* he possesses them without risk and without fear."

74. M. Masson, who makes the same observation, refers here to the pamphlet by A. Schinz; *Rousseau, a*

fore-runner of pragmatism, Chicago, 1909, and to the article by Irving Babbit, *Bergson and Rousseau*.

75. Masson, II, 259. With regard to what he calls the "pygmalionism" of Jean-Jacques: "Rousseau himself made his *Pygmalion* say, "Powerful gods, beneficent gods, gods of the people, who knew the passions of men, ah! you have worked so many prodigies for less cause! See this object, see my heart, and deserve your altars."

76. *Emile*, Book IV (Profession of faith) Cf. Letter to Voltaire of 18th August, 1756: "The greatest idea that I can form of Providence is that every material being is arranged in the best possible way with respect to everything, and every intelligent and sensitive being in the best possible way with respect to himself." (*Corr. génér.*, II, 318). There is no question of a relation to God in all that.

77. "True chastity is in lust," said Luther (1518, Weim., I, 48621) "and the more unclean the lust, the more beautiful the chastity." "Immortal memory of innocence and joy," writes Jean-Jacques. "My voluptuous pictures would have lost all their grace, if the sweet colouring of innocence had been wanting in them."

78. "Conscience," wrote Luther, "ought to have absolutely nothing to do with earthly law, works, and justice." (*In Galat.*, 1535, Weim., XL, P.I. 908, 10-11.) Only civil authority has to trouble about the law and obedience to the law, about Moses and his works. "Legis et bonorum operum alius debet esse usus, valet enim ad disciplinam carnis et ad civiles mores." (Opp. exeg. lat., XXII, 415.) The practice of the law and works belongs to "civil justice," to the civil virtues. (Ibid. XXIII, 221.) That irreducible opposition between *morality* and *legality* was to play a considerable part in German thought.